GO TO HEAVEN

REV. JOHN BOOKO

Order this book online at www.trafford.com
or email orders@trafford.com

Most Trafford titles are also available at major online book retailers.

Print information available on the last page.

ISBN: 978-1-6987-1284-0 (sc)
ISBN: 978-1-6987-1286-4 (hc)
ISBN: 978-1-6987-1285-7 (e)

Scripture quotations marked KJV are from the Holy Bible, King James Version (Authorized Version). First published in 1611. Quoted from the KJV Classic Reference Bible, Copyright © 1983 by The Zondervan Corporation.

Trafford rev. 09/06/2022

North America & international
toll-free: 844-688-6899 (USA & Canada)
fax: 812 355 4082

I get excited that at the age of ninety-nine (2022), I could be going to heaven any day, week, month, or year.

Praise the Lord!

Rev. John Booko Sr. is an American-born Assyrian whose parents were born in northern Iraq. His parents were married in Chicago in 1921, where John was born on November 29, 1922.

He served in the United States Navy during World War II for almost three years as Aviation Machinist Mate Second Class. He gave his life to Christ in the navy and received his call to Christian ministry.

Reverend Booko holds a bachelor of theology degree from Northern Baptist Theological Seminary in Chicago, Illinois, in 1950, and a Master of Arts degree from Northwestern University Graduate School in Evanston, Illinois, in 1951.

He has been an ordained Baptist minister since 1951 and has served in three Michigan Baptist Churches for twenty-four years. In 1975, he founded an interdenominational church, now called Riverside Church, where he served the Lord with his son, Paul, who is the senior pastor.

John and his wife, Burnell, have resided in Three Rivers, Michigan, since August 1963. They have four children, fifteen grandchildren, and fourteen great-grandchildren. His wife went to heaven on April 30, 2010, after sixty-two years of marriage.

He has authored four other books: "Assyria—the Forgotten Nation in Prophecy," The Assyrian Revelation," "No Prayer Power," and "Abundant Blessings." His first book has been translated into the languages of India, Russia, and East Africa. He has traveled throughout the

United States and the world, speaking on the subjects of his books.

He has met with the Israeli prime minister in Jerusalem and Egyptian President Hosni Mubarak in Cairo, where he prayed with him.

HEAVEN

Heaven

Every good thing on earth will be enhanced and advanced to a higher level.
Everything will be better and glorious.

HEAVEN

Redeemer
Relationships
Resource
Residence
Reward (Crowns) MI
Riches (Mt., b)
(Invest in heaven now.)
(3 Ts)
Reservation
Rev. 22; John 14:1–3
(Rejoice your name in heaven.)
Jesus, the way

Heaven - Up North Js 14:B

2 Cor. 5:8 - Absent from the body
Residence (Phil. 3:20)
1. Reunion/Relationships
2. Resting (Rev.)
3. Resurrection of the body
(morning supper)
4. Rewards (1 Pet. 1:4 Lay up Mdb)
(1 Cor. 3; Rev. 14:13; Matt. 25:23)
1 Cor. 15:58 – Five crowns
5. Return to earth for a millennium
6. Reign for 1,000 years
7. Surprise (1 Cor. 2:9)
8. Rejoicing "in Your presence is fullness of joy, singing, dancing, traveling, etc. Not boring!"

Concl. 1. Baby born - crying
Death - laughing
Reservation (John 14:6)

DAVID JEREMIAH

HEAVENLY CITY

1. Rev. 21:2   Holy - no evil
2. 21:17, 18   Gates of pearl
3. 21:19, 20   Foundation of jewels, twelve of the gems
4. 21:18, 21   Streets of gold
5. 21:11, 23   Light from Jesus then Isa. 60:19
6. 22: 2   Tree of life, twelve months, growth in each side of rivers
   Eating with enjoyment
   Therapeutic leaves
22:1, 2   River of life

1,500 miles square - and high
1 Cor. 2:9
Names in the city
Jesus prepared the place for us.
John 14:1–3

No, Our Planet Is Heaven

Germs
Viruses
Diseases
Illnesses
Deformities
Accidents
Robberies
Cheatings
Rapes
Murders
Kidnappings
Terrorism
Pollutions
Poisonings
Drug abuse
Suicides
Sexual abuse
Adult and child abuse
Abortions
Divorces
Debts
Government corruptions
Poverty
Hunger
Homosexuality
Racism
Hatreds
Occultism
Homelessness
Wars

Volcanoes
Earthquakes
Tornadoes
Tsunamis
Hurricanes
Extreme temperatures
Animal attacks
Ungodliness
Unforgiveness
Lack of love
Sins!
We shall be like Christ.

RESURRECTION

Think of the humble caterpillar slowly crawling on earth. Then its life is hidden in the CHRYSALIS, and at least it comes out a beautiful butterfly with its colored wings, flying freely in the air.

That's like our lives.

Citizens of Heaven (Are You?)

Intro
1. Death is the gateway to heaven (2 Cor. 5:8).
2. Better in heaven than on earth (Phil. 1: 23, 24).
3. Jesus is the Way (John 14:1–3, 7).
(Illus. 5.5. Class children asked what to do to get to heaven.
"Good worker? Give money? Be good?" Hands up - "die")

(Spoke in R.C. 7/09) # T-149)

I. The place (Jesus said it's a place, John 14:2.) (see paper)
II. Reasons we want to go to heaven (see paper)

<u>Concl.</u>
1. "Keep your fork."
2. "Who's in heaven?"

(Note - T-149 preached 7/4, 5/9, 3 years ago.)
Leave out "who's in heaven." For R.C. message.
On "Reasons we want to go to heaven," leave out Scripture.

Remember me? (Author unknown)

My name is Gossip. I have no respect for justice. I maim without killing. I break hearts and ruin lives.

I am cunning and malicious, and I gather strength with age. The more I am quoted, the more I am believed.

I flourish at every level of society. My victims are helpless. They cannot protect themselves against me because I have no name and no face. To track me down is impossible. The harder you try, the more elusive I become.

I am nobody's friend. Once I tarnish a reputation, it is never the same.

I topple governments and wreck marriages. I ruin careers and cause sleepless nights, heartaches, and indigestions. I make innocent people cry in their pillows. Even my name hisses.

I am called Gossip. Office gossip. Shop gossip. Party gossip. Telephone gossip. I make headlines and headaches. Before you repeat a story, ask yourself: Is it true? Is it fair? Is it necessary? If not, DON'T REPEAT IT.

Heaven - Ron Lewis

Ezek. 1; Rev. 4; Luke 24:36–43
2 Kings 6:15–17 Elisha, Acts 7 Substance and shadows, Heb. 9:
Time in heaven (Rev. 6:5, 10)
Singing has to have timing "How long" 7:15 day and night later no night. 8:1 "half-hour" 22:2 "Every month" (God is timeless.)
Animals, yes. Creation restored.
Animals saved in the ark.
Rev. 8:13 eagle, 2 Kings 2:11 horses
Rev. 19 horse

Believers in Paradise (Heaven)

"Far better" (Phil. 1:23; Eccles. 7:1)
"Fullness of joy" (Ps. 16:16)
Pleasures forevermore (Ps. 16:11)
(Inexpressible) Unspeakable (2 Cor. 12:4)
Blessed (Rev. 14:13)
Rest (Rev. 14:13)
Precious (Ps. 116:15)
Speaking (Rev. 6:10; 11:15)
Praising (Rev. 19:1, 5; 11:15)
With Christ and joy (Luke 23:43; John 15:11)
Heaven is a place of <u>gain</u> in every way (Phil. 1:20) while they wait for their resurrected bodies.

When in the resurrected body (changed) (all of the above +);
Rewarded
Reign with Christ
Heavenly mansion

Seeing relatives and friends (1 Cor. 13:12)
Seeing angels
Love intensified for God and others
They can ask for updates on things on earth.
We can ask Jesus to deliver messages to our loved ones.
(No communications with the dead)
Perfecting the greatest moments of our past experiences.
Temporary sorrow (Rev. 21:4; 7:17)
Resting but not the rest of inactivity - Continue projects we knew on earth: artists and musicians.
A cloned body until the resurrection
A baby may be allowed to grow up with their parents until full age.

Poems

"I Have a Place in Heaven"
"Safely Home"

Heaven Tours - book

p. 1 - We will find . . .
Unconditional love
Glorious peace
Glorious beauty
Total acceptance
Heavenly music
Praise
Worship
Dancing
Fulfillment
Wonderful light
Super rainbows
Experience greater: wisdom, knowledge, learning, drinks, and food (heavenly manna)
Trust
Joy
Kindness
Health
Strength
Eternal living

My Daily Prayer List

"Call to me and I will answer you."
JEREMIAH 33:3

Heaven, you're in heaven, and my heart beats so that I can hardly sleep . . .

What doing in heaven?

1. Animals will be able to talk. God's new creation will be better. Didn't a donkey once talk? And the snake to Eve?
2. Whatever you can imagine
3. Whatever pleases God
4. Whatever is not boring.
    1) Dancing
    2) Exploring the universe
5. Eccles. 7:1 "better . . . the day of one's death than the day of birth."
6. Isa. 64:4 and 1 Cor. 2:9
7. 1 Cor. 6:2 and shall judge world and angels

CONCL.
Rom. 8:18

Heaven

Where we will
Have jobs and responsibilities and enjoy them (Luke 19:11–27)
Rule and reign with Jesus
Use our creativity
Travel and explore
Be with family and friends
Make new friends
Meet heroes of the Bible
Receive the treasures we have stored in heaven (Matt. 6:19–21)
Receive rewards for what we did on earth
Win a prize (Phil. 3:14)
(Heaven referred to in Bible 583, 256 in NT - KJV)
Christ has prepared a place for us (John 14).
(The hardest part of eternal life is the first eighty or ninety years.)
Your dreams will come true.

Welcome Home to Heaven

"Far Better"

"For Heaven's Sake"

1. Absent from the body, present with the Lord - Jesus knows us by name. Escorted by angels (2 Cor. 5:8)
2. Better personality, mind, knowledge, and memory (2 Cor. 13:12)
3. Meeting others
4. Personal love continues.
5. Glory shall be revealed to us (Rom. 8:18)
6. Fullness of joy (Ps. 16:11)
7. Pleasures forever more (Ps. 16:11)
8. No sorrow or pain (Rev. 21:4)
9. Our gifts will continue and grow: Art, music, science, etc.
10. Our love will grow for God and others.
11. Intermediate state of the body (2 Cor. 5:1) until resurrected body (Moses and Elijah) (Rev. 6:9; 1 Cor. 15:42–55)
12. We shall be like Jesus (1 John 3:2).
13. Space travel - by thoughts
14. Eating for fellowship (Rev. 19:7)
15. Babies and children will grow up with their parents; the elders will grow young.
16. Death is not an end but a beginning in heaven.
    1) While they are sorrowing at our funeral, we are rejoicing in heaven.
    2) When we came into this world, we were crying and others were smelling; at our death, they are crying and we are smiling.

(Joke: Grandpa in a casket in the funeral home. The grandson was told GP was in heaven. Boy: "Did God throw him back down?")

(See picture of Jesus welcoming)
(See funeral book and pocket)
(See Mom C88-E-He)

We will meet our guardian angels and all the other ones.
17. Aborted babies there as adults
18. Reign with Christ (Rev. 5:10; 20:4, 6; 22:5)
(No need to pray for the dead in Bible.)

The Intermediate State

2 Cor. 5:1, 8
God creates a body for us. Those having a vision of loved ones in heaven saw them in recognizable bodies on the Mount of Transfiguration with Jesus. Moses and Elijah (Vision); Temporary bodies till the resurrection
Rev. 6:9, 10 - Souls can take on bodily shapes, but the personalities are the same.
1 Cor. 15:42–44 - Res. bodies; We will travel like Christ did.

Rev 14:13 - <u>resting</u>
Intermediate state?
1. Cloned body? Moses and Elijah (Matt. 21)
2. Waiting for res. body
3. Spirit in heaven, body on earth, and 'til resurrection at second coming
Rev. 11:15 - loud voices and 6:9, 10
<u>Talking</u>

WHAT ARE THEY DOING IN THE INTERMEDIATE STATE IN HEAVEN UNTIL THE RESURRECTION OF THE BODY WHEN CHRIST RETURNS TO THE EARTH?

1. With Christ (2 Cor. 5:8)
2. Resting (Rev. 14:13)
3. Rejoicing (Ps. 16:11)
4. Singing (Rev. 5:9, 10)
5. Worshipping God (Rev. 4:9–11)
6. Serving God (Rev. 22:3)
7. In charge of things (Matt. 25:21)
8. Fellowshipping with others (1 John 1:3)
9. Talking to God (Rev. 6:10)
10. Glorying (2 Cor. 4:18, 19)
11. Looking like Christ (1 John 3:2)
12. Laughing (Luke 6:21)

We shall have a reunion with our loved ones who went to heaven before us. (Mom, Dad, grandparents, siblings, spouse, children, relatives and friends, and some former enemies and saints. Our afflictions work for us a far more exceeding and eternal weight of glory . . . (2 Cor. 4:17, 18).

We will see God our heavenly Father and Jesus Christ our brother and the Holy Spirit our comforter (Rev. 14:13). Our works follow us to heaven. (What works have you done that will follow you?) Hear Jesus say, "Well done, good and faithful servant . . . made a ruler many things, enter into the joy of the Lord" (Matt. 25:23). ("Well done!") (What is done?) Our labors are not in vain in the Lord (1 Cor. 15:58). Death is swallowed-up in victory (1 Cor. 15:54). (Ill. baby cried, adults laughed; adult died, people cried; you laughed.) Jesus has prepared a place for us (John 14:3). Singing and dancing on streets of gold with colorful jewels all around us as seen in Book of Revelation 21, gates of pearl; mouthy ripe fruits

Heaven won't be boring!

CITIZENS OF HEAVEN

By Rev. John Booko

The believers in Christ are citizens of heaven (Philippians 3:20). Our citizenship is in heaven. This world is not our home; we are just passing through.

I have heard and read that heaven is a wonderful place. We should not fear death as it is the gateway to heaven (2 Corinthians 5:8). Absent from the body, present with the Lord. The Apostle Paul said in Philippians 1:23 and 24 that it is far better to be in heaven than on earth.

Here are the top reasons why heaven is better:

Philippians 3:20b, 21: We will have a changed body, a beautiful eternal body that never gets old. No disease or sickness.

John 14:2, 3: We will have a custom-prepared house by Christ.

1 John 3:2: We shall be like Christ (age thirty-three).

Revelation 21:4: God shall wipe every tear from their eyes; there shall be no more death, nor sorrow, nor crying, and there shall be no more pain, for the former things have passed away.

Matthew 25:21; 1 Corinthians 3:14; 2 Corinthians 5:10: We shall receive rewards for faithful service.

2 Timothy 2:11, 12: We shall reign with Christ.

Acts 1:11: We shall be space travelers exploring the universe.

Luke 6:21; Psalm 16:11: We will be filled with joy and pleasures (never boring).

1 Corinthians 2:9: Eye has not seen, nor ear heard, nor entered into the heart of man the things which God has

prepared for them who love Him. Beyond anything we imagine.

Are you a citizen of heaven? You become a citizen by receiving Christ as your Savior who said He is the way to heaven.

Rev. John Booko is the Founding Pastor of the Riverside Church in Three Rivers.

It's Christmas in Heaven

I have always been fascinated with what other people think heaven is like. It is intriguing that whenever artists try to represent heaven or writers try to describe it or movies try to show it, heaven usually comes across as rather boring— the only attraction being that one is not suffering in hell. While not suffering in hell has much to recommend, one does hope that there's more to heaven than sitting on clouds wearing white robes and playing small harps forever and ever!

Representations of heaven in comedies are always entertaining. I remember an episode of "The Simpsons" that has Marge imagining two heavens: one for Protestants and one for Catholics. Protestant heaven is a classy country club with people talking through their teeth. Catholic heaven involves a Hispanic party with Jesus being tossed up in the air with a blanket, and then everyone breaks into a river dance. "Oh dear," says the Protestant, "it appears Jesus has gone native."

A screamingly funny portrayal of heaven comes toward the end of "Monty Python's Meaning of Life." Here, heaven is a giant Las Vegas stage show, complete with chorus girls. The main singer is singing a song proclaiming that every day is Christmas in heaven.

Because these are comedies, they reveal much about ourselves in parodying our ideas of heaven. Being human, our ideas of heaven involve our prejudices as much as they involve our faith. Let's be honest: our ideas of heaven often are about who gets in and who doesn't. We should strive to be better than that.

Generally speaking, I think it is safe to say that for most of us, heaven is an idealized version of life as we know it. I believe this is natural and unavoidable. After all, this life is what we know. And there is much to recommend for this way of thinking about heaven. As Christians, we believe God created all that exists and that it is redeemed and good. Therefore, what our experience of life is can more often than not be our starting point when thinking about heaven.

An interesting phenomenon is what I think of as "The Grass is Always Greener on the Other Side of the Fence" phenomenon. That is, more rural cultures tend to think of heaven as a magnificent city, with streets paved with gold and all that. Whereas more urban cultures will generally conceive of heaven as a pristine forest with friendly wildlife. Rightly considered, both of these ideas can lead to intuitive insights as to what heaven may be like.

One of my favorite metaphors for heaven goes something like this: heaven and hell are identical. In hell, everyone is seated at a lavish banquet. However, no one can eat anything because the silverware is so long that one cannot use it to reach one's mouth. heaven is exactly the same thing. But instead of trying to feed themselves, everyone uses the long silverware to feed each other.

When it comes to me, I personally have two concepts of what heaven is. One is trivial, the other not so trivial. In my trivial version, heaven is me at a really good local coffee shop, drinking really good coffee and eating homemade coconut cream pie for breakfast one day, pecan pie the next. Outside is parked my cream-colored 1965 Rolls-Royce Silver Cloud III with a blue interior. The music inside the coffee shop is always perfect.

In my not-so-trivial version of heaven, heaven is more a state of being and is rather more abstract than physical. Simply put, <u>heaven is ultimately a state of falling deeper and deeper in love with God and everyone else</u>. And this falling deeper in love is never ending.

No one can definitely say what heaven will be like. I would be so bold as to assert that the only thing we can count on is that we will be with God, or perhaps it is God who will be with us. As Jesus said, "I am with you always." And as the name Emmanuel is defined "God with us." Whatever the case may be, as Lady Julian of Norwich has it, "All shall be well, and all manner of things shall be well."

— Br. Martin

CONTACTING THE ABBEY

Mailing address:
St. Gregory's Abbey
56500 Abbey Road
Three Rivers, MI 49093
Telephone:
269-244-5893
9:30 am–11:15 am or 2:30 pm–4:15 pm Eastern Time Monday to Saturday (Please do not telephone at other times or on Sundays or holidays.)
E-mail:
Guest reservations and information:
guestmaster@saintgregorysthreerivers.org
Mailing list:
office@saintgregorysthreerivers.org
Abbot Andrew:
abbot@saintgregorysthreerivers.org

Information about becoming a monk or participating in the July Program:
novicemaster@saintgregorysthreerivers.org
Books and calendars may be ordered, prayers requested, and donations made at our website:
www.saintgregorysthreerivers.org

I WANT to tell you of a wonderful country, a country where there are no tears or heartaches, a country in which there is no sickness, pain, or death. The people who live in this country never get tired. They carry no burdens, and they never grow old. No one ever says good-bye for separations, and there are no disappointments.

In the country of which I am speaking, there is no sin, for no one ever does wrong. There are no accidents of any kind.

It is a country where nothing ever spoils. The flowers never lose their fragrance, and the leaves are always green. There are no thunderstorms, no erupting volcanoes, and no earthquakes. Upon those fair shores, hurricanes and tidal waves never beat. There are no germs or fevers, no pestilences of any kind. The sun never shines, and yet it is always light, for there is no night there. It is never too hot and never too cold. The temperature is exactly right. No clouds ever darken the sky, and harsh winds never blow.

No taxes are paid, and rents are unknown. It is a country free from war and bloodshed.

All are healthy; all are well and strong.

How I know all this? Have I been there? No, I have not yet had the privilege of visiting this wonderful country of which I speak, but others have. And One, at least, who has lived there for a long, long time, has come, and told me a great deal about it. He says it is called

Heaven, and this is His description of it: God himself shall be with them and be their God. And God shall wipe away all tears from their eyes; and there shall be no more death, neither sorrow, nor crying, neither shall there be any more pain." —Rev. 21:3–4.

"Do you not want to go there? Then why not get ready now? It isn't difficult. All you have to do is to open your heart to Jesus Christ, the Lord of the country, and ask Him to come in. Then, when the journey of life is ended, you too will go to this wonderful country and live there for ever more. Will you do it? Do it—NOW?" —Oswald J. Smith

"For God so loved the world that He gave His only begotten Son, that whosoever believeth in Him should not perish, but have everlasting life." —John 3:16.

"But, as many as received Him, to them gave He power to become the sons of God, even to them that believe on His name." —John 1:12.

"For by grace are ye saved through faith, and that not of yourselves it is the gift of God, not of works lest any man should boast." —Ephesians 2:8-9.

"Neither is there salvation in any other: for there is none other name under heaven given among men, whereby we must be saved." —Acts 4:12.

Why Is God Keeping Me Here When I Feel So Bad?

By Billy Graham, Tribune Media Services

Q: I used to be very active in my church, and I taught Sunday school for over thirty years, but now I'm in my 80s and crippled from arthritis and other problems, and I can't even get out. Why is God keeping me here? I'd rather be in heaven. Is it wrong to feel this way? —Mrs. J. W.

It's not wrong for us to yearn for heaven, particularly when the burdens of this life begin to press down upon us. Once, Apostle Paul expressed the same yearning when he was going through a difficult time: "I desire to depart and be with Christ, which is better by far" (Philippians 1:23).

But in the meantime, God has His reasons for keeping us here. Perhaps you can't do everything you once did—but you can pray for others, and you can be an example of Christ's love and peace to those around you. Will your grandchildren or others who know you remember you for your love of Christ, even when life was hard?

May this be a time when you grow closer to Jesus. Someday soon, He will take you into His presence—but until then, take each day as a gift from God and ask Him to help you live it with joy and expectation. God bless you.

This is one of the kindest things I've ever read. I have no way to know who sent it, but there is a beautiful soul working in the dead letter office of the US postal service.

Our <u>fourteen-year-old dog, Abbey, died last month</u>. The day after she died, my four-year-old daughter Meredith was crying and talking about how much she missed Abbey. She asked if we could write a letter to God so that when Abbey got to heaven, God would recognize her. I told her that I thought we could, so she dictated these words:

Dear God,

My name is Meredith. Will you please take care of my dog? She died yesterday and is with you in heaven. I miss her very much. I am happy that you let me have her as my dog even though she got old and sick. I hope you will play with her. She likes to play with balls and to swim. I am sending a picture of her, so when you see her, you will know that she is my dog. I really miss her.

Love, Meredith.

We put the letter in an envelope with a picture of Abbey and Meredith and addressed it to God/heaven. We put our return address on it. Then Meredith pasted several stamps on the front of the envelope because she said it would take lots of stamps to get the letter all the way to heaven. That afternoon, she dropped it into the letter box at the post office. A few days later, she asked if God had gotten the letter yet. I told her that I thought He had.

Yesterday, there was a package wrapped in cold paper on our front porch addressed, "To Meredith" in an unfamiliar hand. Meredith opened it. Inside was a book by Mr. Rogers called "When a Pet Dies." Taped to the inside front cover was the letter we had written to God in its opened envelope. On the opposite page were the picture of Abbey and Meredith and this note:

Dear Meredith,
Abbey arrived safely in heaven.
Having the picture was a big help. I recognized Abbey right away.
Abbey isn't sick anymore. Her spirit is here with me just like it stays in your heart. Abbey loved being your dog. (Since we don't need our bodies in heaven, I can't have any pockets to keep your picture in, so I am sending it back to you in this little book for you to keep and have to remember Abbey by.)
Thank you for the beautiful letter and thank your mother for helping you write it and sending it to me. What a wonderful mother you have. I picked her, especially for you.
I send my blessings every day and remember that I love you very much.
By the way, I'm easy to find; I am wherever there is love.

Love, God.

When we all get to heaven
What a day of rejoicing it shall be
When we all see Jesus
We'll sing and shout the victory!

When talking about heaven, talk about hell. (Jesus did.)

$20.00
200 S. Hooker Ave
Three Rivers, MI 49093
269-279-2672

Rev. 22:12
Rewards and treasures
Rev. 4:9, 10 <u>crowns</u>

Rev. 14:13
Happy are the dead believers and are resting.

Psalm 16:11
The fullness of joy pleasures forevermore.

In Heaven Now

1. Worshipping God, Jesus, and HS
2. Singing
3. Talking to God and others
4. Fellowshipping with Bible characters and others
5. Fullness of joy
6. Pleasures (Ps. 16:11)
7. Resting (Rev. 14:13)

(In white robes while awaiting the resurrection of the body at the second coming of Christ)

(John 14:2, 3) quote

In heaven (Top 10)

RESURRECTION

1. Changed bodies
2. Worshipping and praising God
3. Kings and priests to rule and serve
4. Enjoying our rewards
5. Space travelers
6. Fellowshipping with our families, relatives, our (loved ones) ancestors, friends, and Bible heroes
7. Singing, dancing, and playing instruments
8. Eating and drinking and no bathrooms
9. Fullness of joy and pleasures
10. Learning new things

(1 Cor. 2:9) quote (Ps. 84:1, 2) How truly? . . .

<u>NO</u>
Sickness
Death
Disappointments or sorrows
Sinning
Tears
Takes
Devil
Accidents
Bad memories

When we all get to heaven, what a dap??? that will be!

Heaven

1. Jesus said so (John 14:2, 3).
2. At the death of believers (2 Cor. 5:8)
   1) Spirit in heaven 2) Body in grave
(1) Resting (Rev. 14:3); (2) Speaking (Rev. 6:10); (3) Singing (Rev. 5:1); (4) Worshipping; (5) Praying for us, mostly resting until your body is resurrected from the grave at Christ's second coming (I Thess. 4:16–18)
3. The body changed (1 Cor. 15:51–55; Phil. 3:21; I John 3:2).
4. Rewards (Rev. 22:12; 1 Cor. 3:12–15)
5. Eternal life in the changed body. Describe:
   1) Not boring: Illus. baby in the womb (Eccles. 7:1). Day of one's death better than birth (at birth crying at death laughing) (Ps. 16:11; 1 Cor. 2:9). "Eternity is the highest happiness to believers." (quote)

Concl.
   1. "I can only imagine"
   2. Billy Graham
   3. Christine Nicole
   4. Rom. 8:18, "For 2 recon in the glory" (Ps. 16:11)
   5. Song: "When we all get to heaven . . ."

I can only imagine what it will be like
When I walk by your side
I can only imagine what my eyes will see
When your face is before me
I can only imagine

Yeah

Surrounded by your glory
What will my heart feel?
Will I dance for you, Jesus,
Or in awe of you be still?
Will I stand in your presence
Or to my knees will I fall?
Will I sing hallelujah?
Will I be able to speak at all?
I can only imagine
I can only imagine

I can only imagine when that day comes
And I find myself standing in the sun
I can only imagine when all I will do
Is forever, forever worship you
I can only imagine, yeah
I can only imagine

The best is yet to come.

By Rev. John Booko

(Easter Sunday was celebrating the resurrection of Jesus Christ from the grave.

Isn't that what all the believers in Jesus Christ will experience one day? I believe it! Jesus said so in the Bible.

My son, Pastor Paul, told the following story in one of his sermons at Riverside Church that I would like to pass on to you that shows faith in our own resurrection from the dead.)

There was a woman who had been diagnosed with a terminal illness and had been given three months to live. So, as she was getting her things in order, she contacted her pastor and asked him to come to her house to discuss certain aspects of her final wishes. She told him which songs she wanted to be sung at the funeral service, what scriptures she would like to read, and what outfit she wanted to be buried in.

(Everything was in order, and the pastor was preparing to leave when the woman suddenly remembered something very important to her.) "There's one more thing," she said excitedly.

"What's that?" the pastor asked. She said, "I want to be buried with a fork in my right hand." The pastor stood, looking puzzled at the woman, not knowing what to say. The woman explained, "My grandmother once told me this story, and from there on out, I have always done so. 'In all my years of attending church socials and potluck dinners, I always remember that when the dishes or the main course were being cleared, someone would (inevitably) lean over and tell us to keep our forks for the wonderful dessert that was coming.

So I just want people to see me there in that casket with a fork in my hand, and I want them to wonder, 'What's with the fork?' Then I want you to tell them: 'Keep your fork, the best is yet to come.'" The pastor's eyes welled up with tears as he hugged the woman good-bye.

He knew this would be one of the last times he would see her before her death. But he also knew that this woman had a grasp of what heaven would be like. She knew that something better was coming.

At the funeral, people were walking by this woman's casket, and they saw the fork placed in her right hand. Over and over, the pastor heard the question: "What's with the fork?" And over and over, he smiled.

During his message, the pastor told the people of the conversation he had with their woman friend shortly before she died. He told them about the fork and what it symbolized to her.

So, the next time you reach down for your fork, let it remind you that the best is yet to come for the devoted follower of Jesus Christ.

Rev. John Booko is the Founding Pastor of the Riverside Church.

Citizens of Heaven

By Rev. John Booko

The believers in Christ are citizens of heaven (Philippians 3:20). Our citizenship is in heaven. This world is not our home; we are just passing through.

I have heard and read that heaven is a wonderful place. We should not fear death, as it is the gateway to heaven. II Corinthians 5:8: Absent from the body, present with the Lord. The Apostle Paul, said in Philippians 1:23, 24, that it is far better to be in heaven than on earth.

Here are the top reasons why heaven is better:

Philippians 3:20b, 21: We will have a changed body, a beautiful eternal body that never gets old. No disease or sickness.

John 14:2, 3: We will have a custom prepared house by Christ.

I John 3:2: We shall be like Christ (age 33).

Revelations 21:4: God shall wipe every tear from their eyes; there shall be no more death, nor sorrow, nor crying, and there shall be no more pain, for the former things have passed away.

Matthew 25:21; I Corinthians 3:14; II Corinthians 5:10: We shall receive rewards for faithful service.

II Timothy 2:11, 12: We shall reign with Christ.

Acts 1:11: We shall be space travelers exploring the universe.

Psalm 16:11: We will be filled with joy and pleasures.

I Corinthians, 2:9: Eye has not seen, nor ear heard, nor entered into the heart of man the things which God has prepared for them who love Him.

Are you a citizen of heaven? You become a citizen by receiving Christ as your Savior who said He is the way to heaven.

Dial-A-Prayer 359-6673

Rev. John Booko is the Founding Pastor of the Riverside Church.

Heaven

By Rev. John Booko

Heaven is fun. It is a place of unlimited pleasure, happiness, and joy. You will make known to me the path of life; you will fill me with joy in your presence, with eternal pleasures at your right hand (Psalm 16:11). However as it is written: "What no eye has seen, what no ear has heard, and what no human mind has conceived"––the things God has prepared for those who love him (1 Corinthians 2:9). Then I heard a voice from heaven say, "Write this: Blessed are the dead who die in the Lord from now on." "Yes," says the Spirit, "They will rest from their labor, for their deeds will follow them" (Revelation 14:13).

Heaven is dynamic. It is bursting with excitement and action. It is the ultimate playground. God invented it. It is Disney World, Hawaii, Paris, Rome, and New York all rolled into one. It is a vacation that never ends. It is all inclusive.

We don't lose our identity in heaven. Our changed body will obey the commands of the mind. We will travel faster than light through God's universe.

In heaven, we will experience a whole new variety of sights, sounds, smells, feelings, and tastes. God is a great artist and inventor and creator. Pleasurable sensations are retained in heaven, and God may substitute something better.

Our reunions and relationships in heaven are going to be fabulous with our spouses, children, relatives, and friends. Even our animals (Why not? Psalm 36:6 says God cares for people and animals alike). And don't forget our heavenly assistants, the angels.

"Rest in peace" means going on from what you were doing to greater things—free from worries, suffering, sickness, and pain.

<u>Heaven will not be boring</u>. It will be discoveries and works that never end—with singing, dancing, playing instruments, learning to be an artist, or any other interest.

The highlight of heaven is seeking God! Worshipping and praising Him. He will then have the answers to all of our questions.

Sing this song: "When we all get to heaven, what a day of rejoicing that will be! When we all see Jesus, we'll sing and shout the victory." Jesus is the way.

Rev. John Booko is the founding pastor of Riverside Church.
Dial-A-Prayer*: 269-359-6673*

"Winning the Lord's Award"
II Tim. 4:7, 8

Intr.:

1. Apostle Paul is writing these words at the end of his life to a young man named Timothy.
2. The old soldier of faith looks back and tells this young man what he has done in his Christian life.
3. Here is a victorious saint who has earned his reward.
4. What has Paul done in order to win the Lord's reward?
5. WHAT PAUL HAS DONE TO WIN THE LORD'S AWARD BECOMES COACHING FOR OUR CHRISTIAN LIVES.

   Paul sums up his past life in three Greek figures:

I. A Greek Wrestler ("Fought a good fight")
   1. The word "good" means the beauty of action like a Greek wrestler (Wuest).
   2. The fight is a desperate, straining, agonizing contest.
   3. These pictures our efforts and warfare against sin and evil. (Eph. 6:2: We fight the world, flesh, and the devil.)

II. A Greek Runner ("Finished my course")
   1. "I have run my race." The same figure in 1 Cor. 9:24; Phil. 3:13, 14.
   2. In Acts 20:24, the course was before him; now it is behind him. (The course is the race of life.)
   3. This has the idea of having crossed the finishing line and is now resting at the goal.

4. The Christian is in a race that has a definite course to run, marked out for him. (It's a long race, a weary race, but a glorious race.)

III. <u>A Roman Soldier</u> ("Kept the faith")
1. This means to keep by guarding as a soldier. (Safeguarding the truth)
2. He has been a good soldier of Jesus Christ (II Tim. 2:3, 4; I Tim. 6:12).
3. He, like a soldier who has grown old in the service of his country, is awaiting his discharge.
4. How good to be able to say at the end of life, "I have safeguarded the truth deposited to me"? (Keeping it in the heart as well as defending it against its enemies.)

Concl.:
1. How different these views are from the review which some take of life: wasted life; wicked life; lost power and influence; misery without Christ.
2. The Christian life is a battle, a race, a deposit to be guarded.
3. Paul's use of illustrations from Greek athletics is not finished. He likens himself to the athlete, who, having won his race, is looking up at the judge's stand and awaiting his laurel wreath of victory (8).
4. His award (8)
   1) A crown of righteousness
      (4) For doing right - the reward of righteousness
      (5) A garland of oak leaves or ivy given to the winner (1 Cor. 9:25)

2) Given by the righteous judge
   (1) In this context, this refers to the umpire or referee at athletic games.
   (2) This umpire never makes a mistake and is always fair.
3) At the day of His second coming—the day of His appearing as in 1:12, 18; 1 Thess. 4:16, 17; 5:2; 2 Thess. 2:1–3

5. All this is not for Paul only, but also to all of them who love His appearing.
   1) These are not just believers who are saved but those living in obedience to Him (1 John 2:28).
   2) These are those who by having . . . (v. 7), are looking forward with hope, satisfaction, joy, and love to the day when Christ comes and gives the awards.

(B-3)

"An Open Heaven" (Revision of #241)

Intr.:
1. Christmas time makes us think of heaven.
   1) At the birth of Christ: angels from heaven, the star in the sky
   2) God in heaven loving the world (Jn 3:16)
2. THE COMING OF CHRIST INTO THIS WORLD IN THE FLESH ASSURES US OF AN OPEN HEAVEN (Jn 3:13).
   Why is heaven opened?

I. Heaven opened to give us the Savior (John 1:1, 14). (Chorus: "Heaven came down . . . c78-V)

II. Heaven opened to pour out blessings upon the faith-believing believer (Mal. 3:10; Eph. 1:3; John 15:7).

III. Heaven opened to receive the Savior (Acts 1:11).
1. He who came down from heaven, lived on this earth for about thirty-three years, taught and healed, then died at the hands of sinful men, was raised from the dead, and went back to heaven forty days after His resurrection.
2. This proves His heavenly origin and deity (John 3:13).

IV. Heaven opened to the second coming of Christ (Rev. 19:11).
1. Heaven had opened to give Christ to the world at His incarnation. Heaven was opened to Jesus at His

baptism (Matt. 3:16). Heaven was opened at His transfiguration (Matt. 17:5). Heaven was opened to Jesus at His ascension, and now it is opened to reveal the glorified Christ.

1) The parted heavens show a person seated on a white horse (the emblem of victory) as royal commander, followed by a dazzling army of angels.

2) Here is the commander-in-chief of the host of heaven (King Jesus, Rev. 19:11–16).

2. Here is heaven opened at the second coming of Christ at which time the dead in Christ shall rise, then we which are alive and remain shall be caught up together to meet Him in the air, and then shall we ever be with the Lord (1 Thess. 4:16, 17).

1) Here Christ comes out of the opened heaven to receive us unto Himself.

2) He comes to take us to the heavenly kingdom, not only opened for us but prepared for us!

V. <u>Heaven opened to each who has received the Savior</u> (John 14:6). (c88-E-He-3)

1. Heaven opened to comfort Stephen (Acts 7:56).

1) Just before being killed for Christ's sake, Stephen was given the vision of the opened heaven.

2) A few minutes later, Stephen enters that opened heaven through the stones thrown at him by the mad crowd who had laid their clothes at the feet of a man named Saul of Tarsus.

2. Story of the woman who saw heaven (88-M-2).

<u>Concl:</u>

1. Praise God for an opened heaven. It is open to all—the invitation is still extended through Christ who is the way to the opened heaven from which He came to save us (Matt. 11:28–30; Rev. 22:17).
2. "An old man's letter" about heaven (88-E-He-1)
3. Remember the Revival chorus: "The windows of heaven are open" (c78-V).

Heaven

John 14:1–3

Intr.:
1. Ill. of girls gazing at sky at night (c88-E HE-2)
2. Heaven must be wonderful.
3. It is a comfort to know there is a heaven to go to; death does not end all.
4. Jesus comforted His disciples with the thought of heaven (John 14:1–3).
   Christ tells us several facts about heaven.

I. The Place
1. Heaven is the place where God dwells. "I'm my Father's house (John 14:2a). ("Our Father who art in heaven.")
2. Heaven is the place where Christ has gone (Acts 1:11).

II. The Preparation
1. Made by Christ. "I go to prepare a place for you" (2b).
2. Many mansions of abiding places for us (2a).

III. The Promise
1. "I will come again" (3a).
2. "To receive you unto myself" (3b)
3. "That where I am, there ye may be also" (3c).
   1) With Jesus the Savior - See Him face to face
   2) With all our saved loved ones

IV. <u>The People</u>
1. A prepared people
   1) Must be ready for heaven while on earth
   2) Only those who have been born again (John 3:3)
2. A promised people
   1) Must have the promise of God while living that eternal life is ours (John 3:16; 1 John 5:13).
   2) The promise is given to all who accept Christ as personal Savior (John 3:36). "He that believeth on the Son hath everlasting life . . ."

Concl.: Do you know the way to heaven yet?

It is not through the church, nor ritual, nor works. (Ill. of many going to heaven without things) (c88-E HE-3)

It is only through Christ (John 14:6). None other.

Ingham County Sanitarium 2-18-53 (15M X)

Wils Raden, Lansing 8-13-50 (10 min)

Rewards for Christians

Intr.: *Different from the great white throne for the unsaved (Rev. 20:11–15)

For the saved:

1. *Judgment seat of Christ (2 Cor. 5:10; 1 Cor. 3:11–15) (Salvation not of works, but rewards are.) (Eph. 2:8)
2. Every Christian is a building.
   1) One foundation (11). And cornerstone (Eph. 2:19–22; 1 Pet. 2:4–8). (Not the church, baptism, or good deeds but Christ.)
   2) Building material (12) (that which counts for God and that which does not) W.H.S.G.S.P. such as time, talent, and tithe.
   3) Testing of the materials (13) (By the divine building insp)
   4) Rewards promised (14) (Heb. 11:6; 1 Cor. 15:58)
   5) Losses endured (15)
3. Some may be disappointed in the outcome; some surprised (Matt. 6:1, 2; Col. 3:23, 24).
4. 1 Cor. 9:25–27. Analogy of Greek athlete and Christian by Paul. (For reward, not salvation)
5. There are at least five crowns mentioned in Scripture that any Christian may receive as a reward in heaven. (Rewards on earth too.) (You want any crowns? You want to reign with Christ?)

I. Crown of Life (James 1:12)
   1. For enduring trials
   2. 1 Peter 4:12, 13. For being able to "take it"

*II. <u>Crown of Glory</u> (1 Peter 5:1–4)
   1. For faithful service as a church leader
   2. Consists of vv. 2, 3: "not by constraint" (not as though you had to) "but willingly"; "not for filthy lucre" (not from the motive of personal profit) "but of a ready mind" (freely); "neither as being lords" (domineering) "but being ensamples to the flock" (being models for the people to imitate)

*III. <u>Crown of Rejoicing or Joy</u> (I Thess. 2:19, 20; Phil. 4:1)
   1. For souls won to Christ (For visitation!)
   2. One may share in winning a soul to Christ. (In witnessing, calling, bringing to church)
   3. In praying
   4. Giving

IV. <u>Crown of Righteousness</u> (II Tim. 4:8)
   1. For loving Christ's second coming
   2. An easy crown to receive but few will have it because of neglect
   3. For the triumphant and faithful servant.

V. <u>The Incorruptible Crown</u> – The crown of self-mastery (1 Cor. 9:25–27) (The analogy of Greek athlete and Christian)

Concl.:
   1. Through eternity, we Christians will have with us only the things which we did for God while here on earth.
   2. That may be why Jesus said in Matt. 6:19–21, "Lay not up for yourselves treasures upon earth . . ." (Mark 8:36) (Luke 15 Lazarus)

1) Do you have more money in the bank on earth than in the bank of heaven? "Where your treasure is . . ."
2) "Only one life . . ." (Rev. 22:12)

3. When we see Jesus and fully understand what He has done for us, we will wish that we could have done much for Him.

4. But we still have time to show our love to God by serving Him more faithfully. Not just for the rewards we shall get but for His sake and to hear our Lord say as He did in Matt. 25:21, "Well done . . ."

5. Invitation for salvation (Heb. 12:1, 2) (show of hands), dedication to serving, filling of the Holy Spirit, and healing

6. Commend those who are running their race well.

8/4/57 17 Mxxx
Wakefield Baptist 7/7/57 35Mx
Okemos Baptist 8/12/51 (30 min.)

IV. The City of Heaven

Intr.:
1. "A Country Called Heaven" (88-E-He.T-4)
2. Heaven is spoken of as a country (Heb. 11:14), a city (Heb. 11:16; 13:14), the Father's House (John 14:2), the Kingdom of Christ and of God (Eph. 5:5), and paradise (2 Cor. 12:2, 4).
3. General facts about heaven: N-9, 113
4. HEAVEN IS A PLACE.

We shall see that heaven is a place by what Scripture tells us about its location, description, furnishings, and inhabitants.

I. The Location of Heaven
1. Heaven is somewhere in particular and not just everywhere in general.
   1) Jesus arose in a body of flesh and bone, ascended to heaven, and is now living in heaven in that body (Acts 1:10, 11; Heb. 1:3). (Heaven is a place, or the body of Jesus is nowhere.)
   2) The dead in Christ are now absent from the body and present with the Lord (2 Cor. 5:8).
2. There are three heavens according to the Bible. (No seven heavens.)
   1) First heaven (Acts 14:17). The region of the clouds (The air and clouds on the earth.)
   2) Second heaven (Gen. 1:14). Planetary or starry heaven

3) Third heaven (Neh. 9:6; 2 Cor. 12:2). The heaven beyond the sky. The heaven of heavens and the particular dwelling place of God.

3. Where is the third heaven?

1) It is up. These went up: Christ, Acts 1:9; Elijah, 2 Kings 2:11; Paul, 2 Cor. 12:2, 4. (But which way is "UP"? W-9, 44)

2) It is "in the sides of the north" (Isa. 14:13b). (Quote: W-9, 45, 46)

(Concl.: "See, then, my friends, how very high our calling is. And shall we not value, cherish, and improve it? Shall we throw away our chance for such an eternal home? Shall we slight the offers and opportunities of blessedness like this? Let fortunes pass; let friendships be forfeited; let earthly comforts go unenjoyed; cast honors, titles, crowns, empires to the wolves and bats; but let not the privilege go by of becoming an immortal king and co-retreat with the Lamb in the Golden City of the New Jerusalem." A-3, 511) Seiss 30Mxx

(Concl.: "O, Hallelujah, yes 'tis heaven.

'Tis heaven to know my sins forgiven.

On land or sea, what matters where

Where Jesus is, 'tis heaven there")

(Song #106 "Face to Face")   20 Mxxx

(North is in the same direction from every point on our earth's surface; it is the same from China as from America— the same from the Antarctic as from the Arctic. And north is "up" from everywhere. Whoever heard anyone say "down north" or "up south?"

How significant it is, too, that the geographic and magnetic poles of the earth are always kept pointing north? Who can tell why the magnetic needle in a compass points toward the north star?

When "the glory of Jehovah" visited the prophet Ezekiel, it came with a whirlwind which "came out of the north" (Ezek. 1:4). God says in Psalm 75:2–7, "When I shall receive the congregation I will judge uprightly . . . For promotion cometh neither from the east, nor from the west, nor from the south. But God is the judge."

In the northern heavens, the telescopic camera reveals an apparently empty space where there are no stars, though the region all around is thickly dotted with them. Some astronomers say that this is a "rift in the sky."

What is the meaning of these various scriptures which refer to the north? Could it be that this empty place in the north is the location of paradise?)

V. (II.) <u>The Description of the City of Heaven</u>
<u>Rev. 21:9–22:5</u>

1. Some essential features of heaven:
   1) Rest (Rev. 14:13)
   2) Knowledge (1 Cor. 13:9, 10)
   3) Holiness (Rev. 21:27)
   4) Service (Rev. 22:3)
   5) Worship (Rev. 19:1)
   6) Glory (2 Cor. 4:17)
??? 1. 88-E-He-4 Begin here)
   2. Heaven is spoken of as a country (Heb. 11:14) and a city (Heb. 11:16; 13:14). (Fits city and country folk)
   3. The Heavenly City (Rev. 21:9–22:5) (B-3)
      1) Description of the exterior (10–21)
         (1) Its derivation (10)
         (2) Its location (10)
         (3) Its splendor (11–14)
         (4) Its size (15–21); (C-35, p. 111) 1,500 m square
      2) Description of the interior (22–22:5)
         (1) Its lack of a temple (22)
         (2) Its system of illumination (23)
         (3) Its relation to the earth (24, 25)
         (4) Its holiness (26, 27)
         (5) Its wonderful river (22:1, 2a)
         (6) Its wonderful tree (2b)
         (7) Its absence of sin and its consequences (3a)
         (8) Its glorious throne (3b)
         (9) The conditions under His administration (3c-5)

VI. <u>The Furnishings and Inhabitants of Heaven</u>

(In this series of messages, we have spent the last two messages on heaven. Seeing that it is a place, we have seen what the Scripture told us about its location and description and now its furnishings and inhabitants.)

1. Some of the furnishings in heaven
    1) The heavenly city (Rev. 21:9–22:5)
    2) The tabernacle of the testimony (Rev. 15:5) (Ex. 25ff.)
        (1) That tabernacle in the wilderness was built at a tremendous cost by Moses after the pattern which God Himself gave to him.
        (2) This tabernacle disappears from view, and we hear no more about it. Whatever happened to it is not recorded, except that here, John sees it in heaven.
    3) The temple of God (Rev. 11:19) (But not in the city, 21:22)
        (1) Later, the temple of Solomon was built after the same pattern as the tabernacle but on a greatly enlarged scale (2 Chron. 22:5).
        (2) In this temple, John sees the ark of the testimony (covenant)—that article of furniture, the ark, containing the golden pot of manna, the rod of Aaron that budded, and the tables of stone.
    4) The throne (Heb. 12:2; Rev. 20:11; Ps. 11:4)
    5) The library

(1) Containing many books of records (Rev. 20:12)

(2) In many of these books recorded are the words, deeds, and thoughts of men.

    a. On the record found in these books, men will be rewarded according to their deeds (Matt. 12:36).

    b. Unless these records are destroyed by having your name entered into another book in heaven, all these records will be made public at some future date (Luke 12:2).

(3) There is a book of life in heaven, the "Lamb's Book of Life," which contains all the names of the ones who are saved through putting their trust in Christ as Savior and who have their sins blotted out (Acts 3:19; Isa. 43:25).

2. Inhabitants of heaven

  1) God dwells in heaven in a special sense on a throne with Christ at His right hand (Heb. 12:2).

  2) Seraphim and cherubim (Isa. 6:2; Gen. 3:24; 2 Kings 19:15), special supernatural beings called living creatures.

  3) Angels

    (1) Messengers of heaven

    (2) Ministering spirits (Heb. 1:14)

  4) Saints of God

    (1) All the saved of all ages who have died since Adam

    (2) All who have accepted Christ as Savior from all denominations

(3) All the sinners who have been saved by grace: Adam, Eve, Abel, Noah, Moses, Abraham, Isaac, Jacob, David, Isaiah, Jer. Peter, John, Paul, Stephen, Cornelius, the Philippian jailor, Lydia, Timothy, Augustine, Luther, Wesley, Moody, father, mother, sister, brother, and all the others who have been born again (and all the babies and little children who took a short cut to heaven in by passing this world).

Concl.:

1. And being thankful for this: He will be there. (Ill. Of a youngster, Jon Aldrich, one of the nine children praying: "And we thank Thee, Lord, for all the wonderful things you are preparing for us and the beautiful place it will be. But best of all, Lord, you'll be there.")

2. Heaven, that wonderful place of which we have only caught a glimpse. It's no wonder that God has not revealed to us more of the glories of heaven. We'd be spoiled for this old world, and we wouldn't want to stay here another minute (DeHaan). But there are still souls to be won for him . . .

3. Are you ready for your home in heaven? You can settle the matter now (John 10:9).

#106 Face to face   9-16-79 20Mxx

Three Heavens

(Rev. 22) (Give opportunity to ask a question at the end, in time 6/87.)

Intr.:
1. The Scripture appears to indicate that there are three heavens (2 Cor. 12:2).
2. It is evident that there cannot be a third heaven without also a first and second.
   1) The first heaven must be the atmosphere that surrounds the earth. Reference is made to the fowls of heaven (Hospital 2:18) and the clouds of heaven (Dan. 7:13).
   2) The second heaven may be the stellar spaces for the stars and planets (Gen. 1:14–18).
   3) The third heaven (its location is not clearly revealed) is the abode of God.
      The present divine purpose is to populate the third heaven. It is called glory (Heb. 2:10), and it represents a place rather than a state of mind (John 14:1–3). Those who enter will be "made meet" (qualified) (Col. 1:12).
3. Knowledge of heaven is wholly a matter of the testimony of the word of God. The Bible tells us many times that God is in heaven. Angels live in heaven. God's people who have died are there.
4. These are my testament about heaven and hell, experienced witnesses to the fact of heaven.

2. Christ

Heaven was his abode for all eternity; He discloses more regarding it than does any other person in the Scripture.

1. John 14:1–3. (Finland baby saying Jesus is coming)
2. John 17:24. Prays that we may be with Him (Stephen, Acts 7:54–60)

II. <u>Paul</u>
1. Probably when stoned to death in Lystra; Was caught up to the third heaven (Acts 14:19; 2 Cor. 12:1–4, 7)
2. Upon the basis of actually seeing heaven he could say:
   1) Rom. 8:18, "For I reckon that the sufferings of this present time . . ."
   2) 2 Cor. 4:17, "For our light afflictions which are but for a moment . . ."
   3) 2 Cor. 5:1, 2, "For we know that if our earthly house . . ."
   4) 2 Cor. 5:8, "We are confident, I say . . ."
   5) Phil. 3:20, 21, "For our conversation is in heaven from whence also . . ."
   6) Phil. 1:23, "For I am in a (fix straight) betwist two . . ."
   7) Phil. 1:21, "For to me to live is . . ."

III. <u>John the Apostle</u>
1. Was called into heaven (Rev. 4:1, 2)
2. Described as a place of beauty (Rev. 21:1–22:7). See Rev. 21:4, 5.
3. On the basis of seeing heaven, he had to say in the last prayer of the Bible (Rev. 22:20), "Amen, even so come Lord Jesus."

<u>Concl.</u>

1. These are the same credible experienced witnesses to the fact of heaven. (Others recently)
2. In a few years, some of us here will also be eyewitnesses of heaven.
   1) Heaven is a prepared place for prepared people.
   2) Are you prepared for heaven?
      (1) Ill. "An old man's letter" (88-E-He-1)
      (2) You are <u>prepared</u> for heaven by receiving Christ who is the way to heaven (John 14:6).
3. Here is an amazing thing about the inhabitants of heaven: They are all sinners—<u>saved</u> <u>sinners</u>. (Hell is also filled with sinners, but they are lost sinners—those who did not prepare themselves through Christ.) (Give opportunity for questions here.) (88-E-HE-2)
4. Shall we know each other in heaven?
5. Rev. 22:17a, invitation and command

<u>Heaven Opened</u> (Revised with #475)

Intr.: (Presented outline)

1. The knowledge of heaven is a matter of the testimony of God's word in the Bible.

   1) The Bible tells us many times that God is in heaven, angels live in heaven, and God's people who have died are there.

2. There are experienced witnesses to the fact of heaven.

3. THERE IS AN OPENED HEAVEN FOR EVERYONE. (It is a country with citizens, Ph. 3:20, 2?)

   See examples showing how there is an opened heaven.

I. <u>Heaven opened to give us the Savior</u> (Acts 1:11).

   1. He who came down from heaven lived some thirty-three years on this earth of ours, taught and died, was buried and was raised from the dead, and went back <u>to heaven</u> forty days after His resurrection.

   2. This proves His heavenly origin and deity (John 3:13).

   3. John 14:1–3

II. <u>Heaven opened to comfort Stephen</u> (Acts 7:56).

   1. Just before being killed for Christ's sake, Stephen was given the vision of the opened heaven.

   2. A few minutes later, Stephen entered that opened heaven through the stones thrown at him by the mad crowd who had laid their clothes at the feet of a man named Saul of Tarsus.

III.Heaven opened to commission Peter to witness to the Gentiles (Acts 10:11).

   1. Through this, the door was opened for the Gentiles to become part of the Church.

   2. As it showed Peter that God is no respector of persons (10:34), it shows us that the door is opened in heaven to all who will accept Christ as Savior.

IV.Paul, ESC-2, II; V John, ESC-2, III

V. Heaven opened to the second coming of Christ (Rev. 19:11).

   1. Heaven had opened to give Christ to the world at His incarnation; heaven was opened to Jesus at His baptism (Matt. 3:16); heaven was opened to Jesus at His ascension; and now it is opened to reveal the glorified Christ.

      1) The parted heavens show a person seated on a white horse (the emblem of victory), a royal commander, followed by a dazzling army of angels.

      2) Here is the commander-in-chief of the host of heaven—King Jesus (Rev. 19:11–16).

   2. Here is heaven opened at the second coming of Christ at which time the dead in Christ shall rise, then we which are alive and remain shall be caught up together to meet Him in the air, and then shall we ever be with the Lord.

      1) Here Christ comes out of the opened heaven to receive us unto Himself.

      2) He comes to take us to the heavenly kingdom, not only opened for us but prepared for us!

Concl: ESC-2, Concl. 1–5

1. Praise God for an opened heaven. It is open to all; the invitation is still extended through Christ who is the way to the opened heaven (Matt. 11:28–30; Rev. 22:17).
2. Heaven: "That country . . ." (88-E-He or T-4, or T-1)
3. Heaven's inhabitants (88-E-He-2)
4. Remember heaven is open: "Many may go without . . ." (c88-E He-3).
5. Shall we know each other in heaven?
6. Rev. 22:17

INTR.

Guess what might happen even before this service ends. It's possible. The clouds part, the trumpet of Heaven sounds, and the living Savior could come bursting onto this scene and bring a dramatic and conclusive end to history as we know it.

It might happen, it might not happen, and most of us here might say it probably won't happen today. But the Bible says repeatedly in language that cannot be misinterpreted that Jesus is coming back. Bank on it, trust in it, count on it! Jesus often spoke of it. He said he would die for our sins, be buried, be raised from the dead, and would ascend to the presence of the Father, and at a time no one would know, He would burst on the scene and bring an end to history. History will end when Jesus comes back the second time. (Does this seem far out? But He did.)

When He comes back this time, he will come in power and glory; we will join Him in the clouds. The unbelievers at that time will be hit with terror! (Like you may have seen in movies or TV.)

How many people do you think would believe this?
Fringe elements have made some skeptical by setting dates. (Ill. Oct 28, 1992, set for second coming by a World Watch OM. in South Korea.)

THE ULTIMATE TRIP – MAKE PRACTICAL

INTR. ILL.

    1) Jonathan "not really thought about what it's like in heaven"

    2) "Big Bang" theory: God ??? & hang it happened."

1. Refer to the message on "The World's Greatest <u>Surprise</u>" – The second coming of Christ.

2. Christ is coming to earth again in bodily form. (Quote Bill Hybels intr.) "Another time another place, I'll be swept away."

    1) Just as surely as he came the first time (Surprise as a baby. Surprise as Lord King)

    2) Does the average person think about this?

    3) Jesus said to think about it and plan for it!

3. Christ does a reentry to this earth, and the believer in Christ does a lift-off to meet him in the air (<u>1 Thess. 4:16, 17).</u>

    1) The ultimate trip! (Ill. Challenger and Cape Kennedy excitement)

    (Isn't that fantastic? – The greatest lifted.)

    2) We may never die if He comes in our lifetime. (Think of it!)

4. So, what's it all about?

I. <u>Christ Comes in Glory</u> (Matt. 25:31)

    1. He comes with the believers and for them (Jude 14; 1 Thess. 4:17) (Spirit joins the body.)

    2. Resurrection of the believers (1 Cor. 15:51–55) (The greatest reunion ever. Illus. Reunions on earth)

("One day, I shall see Him face to face." Face to face with Christ my Savior)

3. Satan, the Devil, bound and cast into hell (Rev. 20:10) (after his last fling).
4. A new earth and eternity with our Lord, loved ones, and friends (2 Peter 3:10–13; John 14:3) (forever in heaven)

II. Images of the Afterlife on Earth

1. What comes to your mind when you hear the words: Heaven? Hell? (see #1 over)
2. Where do these pictures in your mind come from? (See #2 over)
3. Can you remember when you were a child what you were taught about Christ coming and then heaven or hell? And about how you got to each place? (Tell of my mother) (Refer to Dramas Drama)
4. Here is what the Bible tells us about it.

III. The Afterlife on Earth
1. No suffering, pain, or death for the believer (Rev. 21:4)
2. A changed body (Phil. 3:20, 21)
3. A perfect life: peace, love, joy, an eternal "Yes" to the goodness of God
4. Got to meet with God, and all the others

CONCL.:
1. But what about those who do not have this ultimate trip with Jesus?

1) There is a hell! Jesus spoke of it more than anyone else, emphasizing the seriousness of our choices in this life. (Here it is.)
2) Matt. 13:40–43; John 5:28, 29; Rev. 20:15
2. Why talk about heaven and hell at the second coming of Christ anyway?
   1) Isn't all this just a way to manipulate people into being good and scare them from being bad? No! (Ill. Of elevator operator)
   2) It's to tell the truth so that we can make wise decisions about life for here and the hereafter.
3. The ultimate trip at the second coming of Christ offers words of hope and words of warning.
4. Are you ready for that ultimate trip?
   1) Do you think it is a mark of arrogance for someone to say, "I know I will go to heaven when the Lord comes back to earth"?
   (1) John 3:16; 3:36
      "Heaven or bust"
   (2) Jesus is the way (road) (John 14:6).
   2) Don't you want to be found <u>faithful</u> and <u>ready</u>?

<u>Prayer and invitation to be ready for the ultimate trip</u> (Drams "Heaven or Bust")

1. What are the first images that come to your mind when you hear the words "heaven" and "hell"?

a. HEAVEN	b. HELL
☐ St. Peter at the pearly gate	☐ devil's pitchfork
☐ streets paved with gold	☐ fire and brimstone
☐ seeing Jesus	☐ home for Hitler
☐ seeing <u>someone</u> again	☐ weeping and wailing

- ☐ wonderful singing and instruments
- ☐ perfect health and body
- ☐ peace and joy
- ☐ surrounded by friends
- ☐ other: <u>seeing God with a beard</u>

- ☐ pain and misery
- ☐ nothingness
- ☐ total isolation
- ☐ other: <u>devil and demons</u>

2. Where do these pictures in your mind come from?

- ☐ books
- ☐ stories heard
- ☐ the Bible
- ☐ art
- ☐ television
- ☐ other: <u>parent</u>

- ☐ church
- ☐ comic strips
- ☐ sermons
- ☐ films and movies
- ☐ dreams

"HEAVEN OPENED"

Pastor John Booko
May 6, 1990

There is an opened Heaven for everyone.

2. Heaven opened to receive <u>our Savior</u>
Acts 1:11

II.   Heaven opened to comfort <u>Stephen</u>
Acts 7:56

III. Heaven opened to commission <u>Peter</u>
Acts 10:11

IV.   Heaven opened to strengthen <u>Paul</u>
2 Cor. 12:1–4, 7

V.   Heaven opened to describe <u>to John</u>
Rev. 4:1, 2

VI.   Heaven opened for the return <u>of Jesus Christ</u>
Rev. 19:11

Shall we know each other in heaven?

The inhabitants of Heaven (88-E-He-2)

Rev. 22:17, the Spirit and the Bride say, "Come."

CH. 1

Intr.:

1. I was born in Chicago in 1922 and born again in 1943 in WW2 in the navy.

   1) A ninety-year-old was asked what you have to do to get to be ninety. He said, "Get to eighty-nine and be very careful."

   2) A ninety-two-year-old had a physical exam, and the doctor in Boston advised him. A few days later, the doctor sees this old guy walking with a beautiful young woman and having a big smile. The doctor stops, and the old man says, "You gave me wonderful advice to get a hot mama and be cheerful." The doctor said, "No, I told you that you had a heart murmur and to be careful."

   3) You are old when you are complimented on alligator shoes when you are (barefoot) in your bare feet.

(Announce my books) (See notes)

2. When you are as old as I am, you think more about heaven and what it is like.

   1) When my dear wife, Burnell, went to heaven in 2010, I asked the Lord to take me soon after to be with her.

      (1) God did not answer that prayer. He said, "I've got work for you to do yet." I said, "Ok, Lord, just keep me healthy and strong to serve you and then take me to heaven <u>healthy</u>." (How exciting!)

  (2) My grandchildren say to me, "Grandpa, you can't go to heaven until you are 120." I have fifteen grandchildren.

3. So, here I am, as your kind invitation to talk about heaven.

4. <u>The place</u> (Jesus said it was a place, John 14:2) – Page 2

II. <u>Reasons we want to go to heaven</u> – Page 3

Rev. John Booko
200 S Hooker Ave
Three rivers, MI 49093

REASONS WE WANT TO GO TO HEAVEN
(See T-149)

(2 Cor. 5:1, 2 Earthly body dissolved) – We will be changed into a beautiful body.

- We will receive a <u>changed body</u> (<u>1 Cor. 15:52</u>; <u>Phil. 3:20, 21</u>), "Humiliation," "Lowly Body"
An eternal body, never getting old. No disease or sickness.
No haircuts, shaving, brushing of teeth or pottie, or makeup.

- We will have a custom-<u>prepared</u> <u>house</u> to live in (<u>John 14:2, 3</u>). (By the carpenter)

* We will be like Christ (<u>1 John 3:2).</u> Be His age. (<u>Ps. 17:15,</u> Awake with his likeness) (Happiest age of Americans over forty was thirty-three.)

- We will meet Bible saints such as Adam and Eve, Abraham, kings, prophets, priests, apostles, and angels.

* We will see and speak to our <u>spouses</u>, <u>children</u>, <u>GC</u>, <u>parents</u>, <u>GP</u>, <u>siblings</u>, relatives, and friends (<u>1 Thess. 4:18</u>) (comfort) (13–17). Those who went ahead will be ready to greet us at the gate. (Beyond the sunset, and glad reunion, v. 4) <u>Song</u>

- We live in a perfect world of glorious light and brightness (Rev. 21, 23). (Time will be no more.) "God gives it light; the lamb is its lamp."

* We will never again suffer from loneliness, boredom, pain, fear, tears, or sorrow (1 Cor. 15:26; Rev. 21:4). "God will wipe every tear from our eyes."

- We will receive rewards for being faithful and fruitful (Matt. 25:21, 23). Make your ruler (1 Cor. 3:14). Will receive the reward (2 Cor. 5:10).

- We will participate in awesome worship and praise (Rev. 5:12–14). They sang these words; (7:9–12) (Reno) she over. We will sing beautifully and perfectly.

- We will see God (Job 19:26). "I will see Him." "We will see Him as He is" (1 John 3:2). We will feel loved.

- We will reign with Christ (Rev. 5:10; 20:4, 6; 22:5).

- We will be space travelers exploring the universe like angels and Jesus (Acts 1:10, 11). (We will travel by thought waves—my thought.)

* We will be filled with joy and pleasure (Psalm 16:11) and "will laugh" (Luke 6:21).

* "NO EYE HAS SEEN, NO EAR HAS HEARD, NO MIND HAS CONCEIVED WHAT GOD HAS PREPARED FOR THOSE WHO LOVE HIM" (1 Cor. 2:9). (We are like in a womb.)

* The best is yet to come! "Keep your fork." (Hold up a fork.)

The next time you reach for your fork, let it remind you that the best is yet to come! For me, to live is Christ and to die is gain.

Rev. 5:11–14

"In a loud voice they sang:
Worthy is the Lamb who was slain, to receive power and
wealth and wisdom and strength and honor and glory and
praise!" (v. 12)
(Singing another verse, 13)
"To Him who sits on the throne and to the Lamb be praise
and honor and glory and power for ever and ever."

THE PLACE OF HEAVEN

Heaven is fun—a place of unlimited pleasure, happiness, and joy (Ps. 16:11; 1 Cor. 2:9; Rev. 14:13) and filled with perfect love.

Heaven is dynamic. It is bursting with excitement and action. It is the ultimate playground. God invented it. It is Disney World, Six Flags, Hawaii, Michigan, and New York all rolled into one. It is a vacation that never ends. It is all inclusive.

We don't lose our identity in heaven (a spiritual body <u>like Christ</u>). Our <u>changed</u> body will obey the commands of the mind. (We will travel faster than light throughout God's universe!)

In heaven, we will experience a whole new variety of sights, sounds, smells, feelings, and tastes. God is a great artist and inventor and creator. Pleasurable sensations are retained in heaven, and God may substitute something better.

Our reunions and relationships in heaven are going to be fabulous (with our spouses, children, grandchildren, parents, siblings, relatives, and friends.) Even our animals. (Why not? Ps. 36:6 says God cares for people and animals alike). (Saved in the ark.) And don't forget our heavenly assistants, the angels! (I've asked God to see my angel.)

"Rest in peace" means (resting going on) from what you were doing to greater things: <u>free</u> from worries, suffering, sickness, and pain.

Heaven will not be boring, ever! It will be discoveries and works that never end—singing, dancing, playing instruments, learning to be an artist or any other interest.

The highlight of heaven is seeing God! Worshipping and praising Him. He will then have the answers to all of our questions.

"When we all get to heaven, what a day of rejoicing that will be! When we all see Jesus, we'll sing and shout the victory!"

"Who's in heaven?" "Judge Not" poem
Illus. A cab driver in Las Vegas witnessed heaven.
The little girl walking with her dad on a starlit night
How beautiful it must be on the other side!

HELL, NO

Intr.

1. Two years ago, I preached on the subject titled, "Go to Heaven."

2. Today, I am going to preach on the subject of "Hell."

   1) "Hell, No" means I won't let you go to hell.

   2) Why do some people say, "Go to hell?" or "The hell with you" and "Hell, no." (They must believe in hell.) (Yes)

   3) If someone ever says to you, "Go to hell," here is a good response: "Hell, no" or "Go to heaven."

   4) Joke about the preacher and deacon and "all wanting to go to hell, stand up."

3. This is not an easy subject to preach about.

   1) I am not going to make it a hellfire sermon either, but it is in the Bible, and I am a Bible teacher.

   2) Did you know that Jesus spoke a lot about hell? He actually said more about hell than heaven. (He does not mean any people to go to hell.)

4. See some of the things Jesus said about hell.

   1) Luke 16:19–31, about the rich man and Lazarus. So . . .

   2) Hell is a place – Jesus ought to know.

      1) Hell is described as a place of everlasting fire (Matt. 25:41, 46).

      2) Hell is a place of punishment. It is a place of punishment for wrongs committed against God, the Father; against Jesus Christ, the Son; against the Holy Spirit; and wrongs committed

against people. (There are <u>consequences</u> for sinning. There are over one million Americans in prison to prove it.) So God is angry at your sin, not at you. He loves you. And He wants you to be saved.

5. <u>Who goes to hell?</u> Rev. 21:8 describes a few of the types of people who go there. (See list)
6. <u>Who doesn't go to hell?</u> Those who:
   1) Repent turn and receive Christ as Savior and are baptized (<u>Acts 2:37b-42</u>). – 12m
   2) Have changed lives (<u>2 Cor. 5:17</u>) (You don't do what you used to, and you do what you used to (show not) not do.) (<u>My testimony</u> of having the hell scared out of me in the navy.) Love Jesus!
   3) Are "born again" (<u>John 3:3</u>) (I got born again to escape hell and have a new life.) Others changed!
   4) Have the promise of <u>John 3:16</u>. Amen? PTL! – 18m

Concl.:
   1. Jesus said a few make it to heaven (<u>Matt. 7:13, 14</u>) (We are among the few.) Thank God!
   2. Some say they are Christians think they will escape hell even though they live like the devil (<u>Titus 1:16</u>).
   3. (So homework) Assignment (<u>2 Cor. 13:5</u>)
      1) Examine yourself – not another (explain)
      2) The Holy Spirit will bear witness for you (<u>Rom. 8:16</u>).
   4. Hell, no! Heaven, yes! (See next page) Heaven where . . .

Our heavenly Father is there (Matt. 5:16).

Our Savior, Jesus Christ, is there (1 Pet. 3:22).

Our dead Christians are there (Eph. 3:15) (our ancestors).

Our reward is there (Matt. 5:12).

Old Testament saints are there (Adam and Eve).

Our treasure is there (Matt. 6:20).

Our trials and tribulations won't be there (Rev. 21:4; 14:13).

Our attainment will equal our desire there (1 John 3:2).

There will be <u>recognition and reunion</u> (1 Thess. 2:19, 20; Matt. 17:3; Luke 16:25; 1 Cor. 13:12).

We shall serve (Rev. 22:3) – Be space travelers.

Rewards will be distributed (Rev. 22:12). (Five crowns: 1 Th. 2:19; 2 Tim. 4:8; 1 Pet. 5:1–4; 1 Cor. 9:25–27; Rev. 2:10)

The <u>longing</u> heart will be satisfied (1 Cor. 2:9).

We will have <u>a changed body</u> (1 Cor. 15:51–55).

It will be better there than anything here (1 Cor. 2:9).

Angels are not bored, so we will not be bored.

We will reign with Christ (2 Tim 2:12).

Heaven, yes; Hello, no!

5. You want in? Pray this prayer in your mind and from the heart:

"Dear God, I am a lost sinner. I don't want to go to hell. I want to go to heaven. I turn from my sinful ways. I turn to Jesus Christ. I receive You as my Savior and Lord right now. Help me to be the person You want me to be! Thank you for saving me. Hallelujah and Amen!"

1) You are now in: Read the Bible each day for how to live the new life and get baptized as soon as you can and tell others of your decision. (Starting point class – Keep coming to church, invite others 10:00 AM, Rm 205.

2) I pray the prayer of thanks for God's love, mercy, and salvation.
3) Offer to remain in the front for any questions you may want to ask me.
4) Prayer partners will also be at the front to pray for any needs you have.
5) Bless you as you go, I love you (23-25 MN).

(2)

Rev. 21:8 KJV

Fearful – cowards
Unbelieving – (not believing in Christ)
Abominable – the disgusting (child molesters, rapists)
Murderers – and terrorists who kill
Whoremongers – sexually immoral
Sorcerers – those rising drugs to produce supernatural effects
(Gr. PHARMAKEUSIN)
Idolaters – worshipping anything before God (money, etc.)
Liars - telling false statements
<u>Let me explain this</u>:
(<u>Repenting</u> or becoming such)
Not "You lie, you fry" but practicing it with no guilt. (No
conscience?) <u>Believer</u> or <u>liar</u>?
<u>So</u>, repent—turn away from these sins which lead to hell!
Now: "And be a follower of Christ and not the devil!"

T-146 - Summary and Scripture

(1)

Intr.: Spoke about heaven two yrs ago. Now "Hell."
Joke about deacon and preacher (means no). No!
This is not easy. No hellfire condemnation.
Jesus spoke more about hell than heaven.
    (Scripture for "Hell, No" message
    July 6, by Pastor John)

Jesus -	Luke 16:19–31 – NIV
Described -	Matthew 25:41, 46 – NIV Depart from me . . . They will go . . .
Who goes?	Revelation 21:8 – NIV - <u>See over</u>
<u>Who doesn't go?</u>	Acts 2:37-42 – NIV
My testimony	2 Corinthians 5:17 – KJV
Changed <u>Loves</u>!	John 3:3 – NIV
	John 3:16 – KJV
You Jew-	Matthew 7:13, 14 – NIV
Phonies -	Titus 1:16 – NIV
Examine -	1 Corinthians 13:5 – NIV
Assurance -	Romans 8:16 – NIV

Concl.:
Hell, no. Heaven yes! Heaven where . . .
You want in? Pray this . . .
You are now in! Read the Bible, baptism, tell others - write them to church. Next Sun. come to STARTING POINT CLASS 10:00 AM, Rm. 205.
Pray and prayer partners - I will remain in front if you have any questions.
Bless you as you go. I love you!

TOP REASONS WE WANT TO GO TO HEAVEN
(Citizens of Heaven)

(Taking a peek into heaven) (Heavenly Daze) (The truth about heaven)

(Burnell went to heaven 4/30/10, nine months after this message) (7/4, 5/09)

<u>Intr.</u>: (Be fluent and enthusiastic in the opening.)

1. Two years ago (2007), I spoke on the subject "Go to Heaven."

    1) I have some more to tell you about heaven.

    2) I have been having a greater interest lately in heaven. (Not like the elderly grandmother who was reading her Bible more than usual and her grandson asking why. She says, "You might say, I am cramming for finals.") (I admit I have been making some preparation.)

2. I hear that heaven is a wonderful place! (Death is a gift that gives us the gift of heaven.) (We should not fear death.) (It is the gateway to glory.)

    1) 2 Cor. 5:8 – key: Spirit <u>absent</u> from the body, Spirit <u>present</u> with the Lord. (Got it?)

       (Joke: Grandson at funeral home viewing departed grandpa.

       Mother comforts her little boy saying, "Grandpa went to heaven to be with the Lord." Grandson looks at grandpa in the casket and says, "Did the Lord throw him back down?") (You are alive in your spirit.)

Look at: 2) Phil. 1:23, 24 – Say, "Better by far." (You want me to stick around longer.)

Pastor Rick Warren quote on the Purpose of Life (88-E-He): "In a nutshell, life is preparation for eternity . . . and God wants us to be with Him in heaven . . . I may live to 60 to 100 years on earth, but I am going to spend trillions of years in eternity. This is the warm-up act - the dress rehearsal."

3. We are going to take a peek at heaven.
   1) Right now, heaven is an in-between place waiting for our resurrected body. (Our spirit only is there. It is like booking a flight to Hawaii and having a stop or layover in California.) (An intermediate heavenly place)
      (1) The spirit is resting there (Rev. 14:13). (Luke 16:25 "Lazarus was comforted.")
      (2) Our spirit is speaking (Rev. 6:10).
      (3) Our spiritual self is full of joy and eternal pleasure (Ps. 16:11).
   2) <u>At Christ's second coming,</u> we received our changed body from the grave (1 Cor. 15:51, 52; 1 Thess. 4:13–17).
   3) Then, when Christ comes to earth, there is the millennium (Rev. 20:4)—the one-thousand-year reign of Christ on earth.
4. Then <u>get ready for the new heaven</u> (Rev. 21:1).
   <u>Why would you want to go to heaven?</u>

<u>TOP REASONS WE WANT TO GO TO HEAVEN -</u> <u>With resurrected bodies</u>
(Scriptures in parenthesis are not printed.)

1•   We will receive a changed body, Phil. 3:20, 21. (A beautiful changed body. An eternal body, never getting old. No disease or sickness.
No haircuts, shaving, brushing of teeth or pottie, or putting on makeup.)

2•   We will have a custom-prepared house to live in, John 14:2, 3.

3*   We will be like Christ, 1 John 3:2. (<u>Be His age.</u>) (Phil. 3:21) (Like after his resurrection; Acts 1:10, 11 not printed)

4   We will meet Bible saints such as Adam and Eve, Abraham, kings, prophets, priests, apostles, and angels. (Matt. 8:11) Not printed

5*   We will see and speak to our relatives and friends. (1 Thess. 4:13–17) Not printed (They will be ready to greet us.) (1 Cor. 13:12) (Remember this scripture, "We shall be together.")

(Hi, Mom. HI, Dad. Hi, Grandpa. Hi, Grandma. Where is Uncle Serge? Around. ("When we all get to heaven, what a day of rejoicing, it will be!")

6*   We will never again suffer from loneliness, boredom, pain, fear, tears, or sorrow, Rev. 21:4. (beautiful)

7• We will receive rewards for being faithful and fruitful. (Rev. 19:8) Matt. 25:21; 1 Cor. 3:14; 2 Cor. 5:10. (These are crowns to get.) (All your giving, all your serving—all your talents for God will payoff.)

8• We will participate in awesome worship and praise. (You can read it in Rev. 5.) (Rev. 5:8–13) We will sing beautifully and perfectly. Also play instruments. V.8, 4 living creatures and 24 elders. Sang V.9, 10 (and harps). Angels sing, 11, 12. Everyone sings, 13. Words: 9, 10, 12, 13.)

9• We will see God! (Job 19:26; 1 John 3:2) (We will feel loved.)

10• We will reign with Christ. (Rev. 5:10; 20:4, 6; 22:15.) Not printed 2 Tim. 2:11, 12 (We will get crowns and authority.)

11• We will be space travelers exploring the universe like angels and Jesus. Acts 1:11. We will travel (by thoughts waves) faster than the speed of light—186,000 per sec.

12• We will be filled with joy and pleasure, Luke 6:21; Ps, 16:11. Never bored. A laughing place. God laughs.

13* Indescribable, 1 Cor. 2:9 (Awesome, amazing, wonderful, etc.)

14*   <u>We will have been saved from going to hell</u>. (<u>Thank you, Jesus!</u>) (8M & 9 = <u>17M</u>)

<u>Concl.</u>: (Let's give the Lord a hand for heaven!)
1. Our citizenship is in heaven, Phil. 3:20.
    1) We have dual citizenship. (Song: "This world is not my home . . .")
    2) Are you a <u>citizen of heaven</u>? If not, <u>Do you want to become one?</u>
    3) Be born into the kingdom of heaven by being "born again."
       (1) Turn away from sinful ways.
       (2) Turn to Christ to receive Him and follow Him.

<u>With heads bowed:</u>
(<u>Ask</u>: "How many of you want to receive Christ as your Savior now and become a citizen of heaven?" If a response is a show of hands, <u>then</u> <u>put</u> your hands down and say these words in your hearts.)
Close with this:
2. Rom 8:18 KJV "For reckon . . ." (Say, "I reckon.")

<u>Bow your head and say in your heart:</u>
"Lord Jesus,

I turn away from my sinful ways,

I turn to you, Jesus,

And receive you as my Savior.

Thank you for the forgiveness of all my sins,

And the promise of heaven for me. Amen."

Commend and <u>applaud</u> those who prayed this.

3. Who's in heaven? <u>Poem</u> - <u>read</u>

Who's in Heaven?

I was shocked, confused, bewildered
as I entered Heaven's door,
Not by the beauty of it all,
by the lights, or its decor.

But it was the folks in Heaven
who made me sputter and gasp-
the thieves, the liars, the sinners,
the alcoholics, the trash.

There stood the kid from seventh grade
who swiped my lunch money twice.
Next to him was my old neighbor
who never said anything nice.

Herb, who I always thought
was rotting away in hell,
was sitting pretty on cloud nine,
looking incredibly well.

I nudged Jesus, "What's the deal?
I would love to hear Your take.
How'd all these sinners get up here?
God must've made a mistake.

And why's everyone so quiet,
so somber? Give me a clue."
"Hush, child," said He. "They're all in shock."
No one thought they'd see you."
(Judge not!)

And we may not know all of what heaven is like, but we
do know one thing for sure: Our Lord is there, and that is
enough! (Prayer or "God bless")

<u>Intr.:</u> (NKJV unless noted otherwise)
2 Cor. 5:8 – We are confident, I say, and willing rather to be absent from the body, and to be present with the Lord.

Phil. 1:23, 24 – I am torn between the two: I desire to depart and be with Christ, which is better by far, but it is more necessary for you that I remain in the body. NIV

Rev. 14:13 – Blessed are the dead that die in the Lord . . . "Yes, says the Spirit, that they may rest from their labors and their works do follow them."

Rev. 6:10 – The souls . . . called out in a loud voice… NIV

Psalm 16:11 – In Your presence is fullness of joy; at Your right hand there are pleasures for evermore.

1 Cor. 15:51, 52 – Behold, I show you a mystery; we shall not all sleep, but we shall be changed, in a moment, in the twinkling of any eye, at the last trumpet; for the trumpet shall sound, and the dead shall be raised incorruptible, and we shall be changed.

1 Thess. 4:13-17 – But I do not want you to be ignorant, brethren, concerning those who have fallen asleep, lest you sorrow as others who have no hope. For if we believe that Jesus died and rose again, even so God will bring with Him those who sleep in Jesus. For we say this to you by the word of the Lord, that we who are alive and remain until the coming of the Lord will by no means precede those who are asleep. For the Lord Himself will descend from heaven with a shout, with the voice of an archangel, and with the trumpet of God. And the dead in Christ will rise first. Then

we which are alive and remain shall be caught up with them in the clouds to meet the Lord in the air, and thus we shall always be with the Lord. (Wow! Hallelujah!)

Rev. 20:4b – And they lived and reigned with Christ for a thousand years.

Rev. 21:1 – And I saw a new heaven and a new earth, for the first heaven and the first earth had passed away.

TOP REASONS WE WANT TO GO TO HEAVEN

1. Phil. 3:20b, 21a – The Lord Jesus Christ will transform our lowly body so that it may be conformed to His glorious body.
2. John 14:2, 3 – Jesus said, "In My Father's house are many mansions, if it were not so, I would have told you. I go to prepare a place for you . . . that where I am, there you may be also."
3. I John 3:2 – Beloved, now we are the children of God; and it has not yet been revealed what we shall be; but we know that when He is revealed, we shall be like Him, for we shall see Him as He is.
6. Rev. 21:4 – God shall wipe away every tear from their eyes; there shall be no more death, nor sorrow, nor crying; and there shall be no more pain, for the former things have passed away.
   Matt. 25:21 – His Lord said to him, "Well done, good and faithful servant; you were faithful over a few things, I will make you <u>ruler</u> over many things. Enter into the joy of your Lord."

7. 1 Cor. 3:14 – If anyone's work which he has built upon endures, he will receive a reward.

    2 Cor. 5:10 – For we must all appear before the judgment seat of Christ, that each one may receive the things done in the body, according to what he has done.

10. 2 Tim. 2:11, 12 – For if we died with Him, we shall also live with Him. If we endure, we shall also reign with Him.

11. Acts 1:11 – This same Jesus who was taken up from you to heaven, will so come in like manner as you saw Him go into heaven.

12. Luke 6:21 – Blessed are you who weep now, for you shall laugh.

    Psalm 16:11 – In His presence is fullness of joy.

13. 1 Cor. 2:9 – Eye has not seen, nor ear heard, nor have entered into the heart of man the things which God has prepared for those who love Him.

Concl.:

Phil. 3:20 – For our citizenship is in heaven, from which we also eagerly wait for the Savior, the Lord Jesus Christ.

Rom. 8:18 – For I reckon that the sufferings of this present time are not worthy to be compared with the glory which shall be revealed in us. KJV

<u>GO TO HEAVEN</u> (is the title of my message today. Did you get the implication? Tell people where to go!)

I. There really is a place called heaven!
  1. How do we know?
    1) Someone was there and came to earth and told that it is a place - Jesus (<u>John 14:2, 3</u>; <u>Acts 1:10, 11</u>)
    2) Apostle Paul (<u>2 Cor. 12:2–4</u>) (Three heavens: 1. clouds, 2. planets, 3. God up north)
    3) Apostle John (<u>Rev. 21:1–4</u>)
    4) Angels appear from heaven to earth all the time.
    5) People have been declared dead and came back to life saying they saw heaven and even were there. (Don Piper book "90 Minutes in Heaven.")
  2. Heaven is so attractive that nothing can compare to its beauty.
    Gold streets
    Pearly gate
    St. Peter
    Seeing God, Jesus, and others
    Singing, peace, and joy
    Perfect body and health
    1) What are the first images that come to your mind when you hear the word "heaven"? (Ask for responses from the audience and repeat them.) (Tell them that later on, "I am going to have a question-and-answer time if they have questions.") (Humor: St. Peter and ex-wife at Pearly gates to spell to get in)

2) Illus. of a father and little daughter under starlights. (If the bottom side of heaven is so beautiful, how wonderful is the other side?) (Jesus has been preparing the place for us for 2,000 yrs.)

3) 1 Cor. 2:9 Eye has not seen . . . (not boring!)

II. Why be afraid of death? (Dying is not for sissies!)

1. Death is when your spirit leaves your body and goes to heaven as a saved believer (James 2:26).

2. 2 Cor. 5:8, absent from the body, present with the Lord

3. The Bible says the day of one's death is better than the day of birth (Eccles. 7:1).

(See what Apostle Paul said about it in Phil: 23, 24; 21.)

4. Ill. of a baby in the womb and us in this earth's womb

5. One generation of followers of Christ will not ever see death.

1) At the second coming of Christ (1 Thess. 4:16, 17).

2) Change bodies (1 Cor. 15:51, 52; Phil. 3:20, 21)

Concl.:

1. Question and answer time. (If not enough questions are asked, speak on what the departed believers are doing. See separate paper.) (Over) (About 10 min.) (Tell that I will stay in front for further questions at the end of the service.)

2. Can you be sure you will go to heaven? Yes!

1) Jesus is the way (John 14:6).

2) Jesus gave us the promise (John 3:16).

3) <u>1 John 5:13</u>, "know" say "know." (Not "no")
4) Give an invitation for assurance in heaven. ASK: How many of you know that if you died today, you would go to heaven? How many are not sure but want to be sure?
5) Prayer of salvation and thanks. The best is yet to come: "Go to Heaven."

<u>What are they doing?</u> In intermediate state (until resurrection)

1. With Christ (not boring)
2. Resting (Rev. 14:13)
3. Rejoicing (Ps. 16:11)
4. Singing (Rev. 5:9, 10)
5. Worshipping God (Rev. 4:9–11)
6. Serving God (Rev. 22:3)
7. In charge of things (Matt. 25:21)
8. Fellowshipping with others (1 John 3:1)
9. Glory (2 Cor. 4:18, 19)
10. We shall be like him. (After the resurrection of our bodies, we will have a "ball.") (On man earth)

<u>Heaven</u>

1. Reunion (1 Cor. 13:12)
   "Then shall we know."
2. Rewards
   "Great is your reward . . ."
   "Reward is with Him."
   Clothes in Rev. 19:8 are according to Your works.

"Heaven - Our Enduring Fascination With the Afterlife"
Lisa Miller

SCRIPTURE NKJV FOR MESSAGE ON HEAVEN

(This is Heaven.)

<u>John 14:2, 3</u> – In my Father's house are many mansions, if it were not so I would have told you. I go to prepare a place for you. And if I go and prepare a place for you, I will come again and receive you to Myself, that where I am, there you may be also.

<u>Acts 1:10, 11</u> – And while they looked steadfastly toward heaven as He went up, behold two men stood by them in white apparel. Who also said, "Men of Galilee, why do you stand gazing into heaven? This same Jesus, who was taken up from you into heaven, will so come in like manner as you saw Him <u>go into heaven.</u>"

<u>2 Cor. 12:2–4</u> – I know a man in Christ who fourteen years ago . . . was caught up to the third heaven . . . and heard inexpressible words . . .

<u>Rev. 21:1–4</u> – And I saw a new heaven and a new earth . . . Then, I, John saw the holy city, New Jerusalem, coming down out of heaven from God . . . God Himself will be with them and be their God. And God will wipe away every tear from their eyes; there shall be no more death, nor sorrow, nor crying. There shall be no more pain, for the former things have passed away.

<u>1 Cor. 2:9</u> – Eye has not seen, nor ear heard, nor have entered into the heart of man the things which God has prepared for those who love Him.

<u>James 2:26</u> – The body without the spirit is dead.

<u>2 Cor. 5:8</u> – Absent from the body and to be present with the Lord.

<u>Eccles. 7:1</u> – The day of death better than the day of birth.

<u>Phil. 1:23, 24</u> – I am hard pressed between the two; having a desire to depart and be with Christ, which is far better. Nevertheless to remain in the flesh is more needful for you. <u>V.21</u> – For to me to live is Christ, and to die is gain.

<u>I Thess. 4:16, 17</u> – The Lord Himself will descend from heaven with a shout, with the voice of an archangel, and with the trumpet of God. And the dead in Christ will rise first. Then we who are alive and remain shall be caught up together with in the clouds to meet the Lord in the air.

Change Bodies
<u>1 Cor. 15:51, 52</u> – Behold, I tell you a mystery: We shall not all sleep, but we shall all be changed – In a moment, in the twinkling of an eye, at the last trumpet. For the trumpet will sound and the dead will be raised incorruptible and we shall be changed.

<u>Phil. 3:20, 21</u> – For our citizenship is in heaven, from which we also eagerly wait for the Savior, the Lord Jesus Christ. Who will transform our lowly body that it may be conformed to his glorious body.

Q & A time – 10 min.

<u>John 14:6</u> – Jesus said to him, "I am the way, the truth, and the life. No one comes to the Father except through Me."

John 3:16 – For God so loved the world, that He gave His only begotten Son, that whoever believes in Him should not perish but have everlasting life.

I John 5:13 – These things have I written to you who believe in the name of the Son of God, that you may know that you have eternal life.

Reasons We Want to Go to Heaven

BY REV. JOHN BOOKO

- We will receive a changed body (1 Cor. 15:52; Phil. 3:20, 21). An eternal body, never getting old. No disease or sickness. No haircuts, shaving, brushing of teeth, etc.
- We will have a custom-prepared house to live in (John 14: 2, 3).
- We will meet Bible saints such as Adam and Eve, Abraham, prophets, priests, apostles, and angels (Matt. 8:11).
- We live in a perfect world of glorious light and brightness (Rev. 21, 22). Time will be no more.
- We will never again suffer loneliness, boredom, pain, fear, sorrow, or suffering (1 Cor. 15:26; Rev. 21:4).
- We will receive rewards for being faithful and fruitful (Matt. 25:21, 23; 1 Cor. 3:14; 2 Cor. 5:10).
- We will participate in awesome worship and praise (Rev. 5:11–14; 7:9–12). We will sing beautifully and perfectly.
- We will see God (Job 19:26; 1 John 3:2). We will feel loved.
- We will reign with Christ (Rev. 5:10; 20:4, 6; 22:15).
- We will be space travelers exploring the universe like angels (Acts 1:10, 11).
- We will be filled with joy and pleasure (Psalm 16:11).

"No eye has seen, no ear has heard, no mind has conceived what God has prepared for those who love him" (1 Cor. 2:9).

Rev. John Booko is the founding pastor of the Riverside Church.

REASONS WE WANT TO GO TO HEAVEN

- We will receive a changed body (1 Cor. 15:52; Phil. 3:20, 21). An eternal body, never getting old. No disease or sickness. No haircuts, shaving, brushing of teeth or pottie, etc.

- We will have a custom-prepared house to live in (John 14:2, 3).

* We will be like Christ (1 John 3:2). Be His age.

- We will meet Bible saints such as Adam and Eve, Abraham, prophets, priests, apostles, and angels (Matt. 8:11).

* We will see and speak to our relatives and friends (1 Thess. 4:13–17). They will be ready to greet us at the gate.

- We Live in a perfect world of glorious light and brightness (Rev. 21, 22). Time will be no more.

* We will never again suffer from loneliness, boredom, pain, fear, tears, or sorrow (1 Cor. 15:26; Rev. 21:4).

- We will receive rewards for being faithful and fruitful (Matt. 25:21, 23; 1 Cor. 3:14; 2 Cor. 5:10).

- We will participate in awesome worship and praise (Rev. 5:11–14; 7:9–12). We will sing beautifully and perfectly.

- We will see God (Job 19:26; 1 John 3:2). We will feel loved.

- We will reign with Christ (Rev. 5:10; 20:4, 6; 22: 5).

- We will be space travelers exploring the universe like angels (Acts 1:10, 11). We will travel by thought waves.

* We will be filled with joy and pleasure (Psalm 16:11).

"NO EYE HAS SEEN, NO EAR HAS HEARD, NO MIND HAS CONCEIVED WHAT GOD HAS PREPARED FOR THOSE WHO LOVE HIM" (1 Cor. 2:9).

Intr.:

1. I was born in Chicago in 1922 and born again in 1943 in WW2 in the navy.

    1) A ninety-year-old was asked what you have to do to get to be ninety. He said, "Get to eighty-nine and be very careful."

    2) A ninety-two-year-old had a physical exam, and the doctor in Boston advised him. A few days later, the doctor sees this old guy walking with a beautiful young woman and having a big smile. The doctor stops, and the old man says, "You gave me wonderful advice to get a hot mama and be cheerful." The doctor said, "No, I told you that you had a heart murmur and to be careful."

    3) You are old when you are complimented on alligator shoes when you are barefoot.

2. When you are as old as I am, you think more about heaven and what it is like.

    1) When my dear wife, Burnell, went to heaven in 2010, I asked the Lord to take me soon after to be with her.

        (1) God did not answer that prayer. He said, "I've got work for you to do yet." I said, "OK, Lord, just keep me healthy and strong to serve you and then take me to heaven healthy."

        (2) My grandchildren say to me "Grandpa, you can't go to heaven until you are 120." I have fifteen grandchildren.

3. So, here I am (as your kind invitation) to talk about heaven.

I. <u>The place</u> (Jesus said it was a place, John 14:2) - p. 2

II. <u>Reasons we want to go to heaven.</u> - p. 3

THE PLACE OF HEAVEN

Heaven is fun—a place of unlimited pleasure, happiness, and joy (Ps. 16:11; 1 Cor. 2:9; Rev. 14:13) and filled with perfect love.

Heaven is dynamic. It is bursting with excitement and action. It is the ultimate playground. God invented it. It is Disney World, Six Flags, Hawaii, Michigan, and New York all rolled into one. It is a vacation that never ends. It is all inclusive.

We don't lose our identity in heaven (a spiritual body like Christ). Our changed body will obey the commands of the mind. (We will travel faster than light throughout God's universe.)

In heaven, we will experience a whole new variety of sights, sounds, smells, feelings, and tastes. God is a great artist and inventor and creator. Pleasurable sensations are retained in heaven, and God may substitute something better.

Our reunions and relationships in heaven are going to be fabulous (with our spouses, children, grandchildren, parents, siblings, relatives, and friends.) Even our animals. (Why not? Ps. 36:6 says God cares for people and animals alike). (Saved in the ark.) And don't forget our heavenly assistants, the angels!

"Rest in peace" means going on from what you were doing to greater things: free from worries, suffering, sickness, and pain.

Heaven will not be boring, ever! (Will it?) It will be discoveries and works that never end—with singing, dancing, playing instruments, learning to be an artist, or any other interest.

The highlight of heaven is seeing God! Worshipping and praising Him. He will then have the answers to all of our questions.

"When we all get to heaven, what a day of rejoicing that will be! When we all see Jesus, we'll sing and shout the victory!"

The best is yet to come for the follower of Christ
(Read about the fork.)

REASONS WE WANT TO GO TO HEAVEN
(see T-149)

- We will receive a changed body. "We will be changed in a beautiful body" (1 Cor. 15:52; Phil. 3:20, 21). An eternal body, never getting old. No disease or sickness. No haircuts, shaving, brushing of teeth or pottie, etc. or makeup.

- We will have a custom prepared house to live in (John 14:2, 3).

* We will be like Christ (1 John 3:2) Be His age. (Ps. 17:15, his likeness) (Happiest age of Americans over forty was thirty-three.)

- We will meet Bible saints such as Adam and Eve, Abraham, kings, prophets, priests, apostles, and angels (Matt. 8:11).

* We will see and speak to our spouses, children, GC, parents, GP, siblings, relatives, and friends) (1 Thess. 4:13–17). Those who went ahead will be ready to greet us at the gate. (Beyond the sunset and glad reunion, v. 4)

- We live in a perfect world of glorious light and brightness (Rev. 21, 23). (Time will be no more.) "God gives it light; the lamb is its lamp."

* We will never again suffer from loneliness, boredom, pain, fear, tears, or sorrow (1 Cor. 15:26; Rev. 21:4). "God will wipe every tear from our eyes."

- We will receive rewards for being faithful and fruitful (Matt. 25:21, 23; 2 Cor. 3:14; 2 Cor. 5:10).

- We will participate in awesome worship and praise (Rev. 5:11–14; 7:9–12). We will sing beautifully and perfectly. Sang these words (Read).

- We will see God (Job 19:26; 1 John 3:2). We will feel loved. "I will see Him." "We will see Him as He is."

- We will reign with Christ (Rev. 5:10; 20:4, 6; 22: 5).

- We will be space travelers exploring the universe like angels and Jesus (Acts 1:10, 11). (We will travel by thought waves.)

* We will be filled with joy and pleasure (Ps. 16:11) and will laugh (Luke 6:21).

* The best is yet to come! "Keep your fork."

"NO EYE HAS SEEN, NO EAR HAS HEARD, NO MIND HAS CONCEIVED WHAT GOD HAS PREPARED FOR THOSE WHO LOVE HIM" (1 Cor. 2:9)

The Best Is Yet to Come

By Rev. John Booko

Easter Sunday was celebrating the resurrection of Jesus Christ from the grave.

Isn't that what all the believers in Jesus Christ will experience one day? I believe it! Jesus said so in the Bible.

My son, Pastor Paul, told the following story in one of his sermons at Riverside Church that I would like to pass on to you that shows faith in our own resurrection from the dead.

There was a woman who had been diagnosed with a terminal illness and had been given three months to live. So, as she was getting her things in order, she contacted her pastor and asked him to come to her house to discuss certain aspects of her final wishes. She told him which songs she wanted to be sung at the funeral service, what scriptures she would like to be read, and what outfit she wanted to be buried in.

Everything was in order, and the pastor was preparing to leave when the woman suddenly remembered something very important to her. "There's one more thing," she said excitedly.

"What's that?" the pastor asked. She said, "I want to be buried with a fork in my right hand." The pastor stood, looking puzzled at the woman, not knowing what to say. The woman explained, "My grandmother once told me this story, and from there on out, I have always done so. 'In all my years of attending church socials and potluck dinners, I always remember that when the dishes or the main course were being cleared, someone would (inevitably) lean over and tell us to keep our forks for the wonderful dessert that was coming.

So I just want people to see me there in that casket with a fork in my hand, and I want them to wonder 'What's with the fork?' Then I want you to tell them: 'Keep your fork, the best is yet to come.'" The pastor's eyes welled up with tears as he hugged the woman good-bye.

He knew this would be one of the last times he would see her before her death. But he also knew that this woman had a grasp of what heaven would be like. She knew that something better was coming.

At the funeral, people were walking by this woman's casket, and they saw the fork placed in her right hand. Over and over, the pastor heard the question "What's with the fork?" And over and over he smiled.

During his message, the pastor told the people of the conversation he had with their woman friend shortly before she died. He told them about the fork and what it symbolized to her.

So, the next time you reach down for your fork, let it remind you that the best is yet to come for the devoted follower of Jesus Christ.

Rev. John Booko is the Founding Pastor of the Riverside Church.

Who's in Heaven?

I was shocked, confused, bewildered
as I entered Heaven's door,
Not by the beauty of it all,
by the lights, or its decor.

But it was the folks in Heaven
who made me sputter and gasp -
the thieves, the liars, the sinners,
the alcoholics, the trash.

There stood the kid from seventh grade
who swiped my lunch money twice.
Next to him was my old neighbor
who never said anything nice.

Herb, who I always thought
was rotting away in hell,
was sitting pretty on cloud nine,
looking incredibly well.

I nudged Jesus, "What's the deal?
I would love to hear Your take.
How'd all these sinners get up here?
God must've made a mistake.

And why's everyone so quiet,
so somber? Give me a clue."
"Hush, child," said He. "They're all in shock."
No one thought they'd see you."
(Judge not!)

The Way to Heaven

By Rev. John Booko

Apostle Thomas, commonly known as "doubting" Thomas, asked Christ, "How can we know the way to heaven?" Jesus answered him with these words: "I am the way, the truth, and the life; no one comes to the Father but by Me" (John 14:6).

I wonder what answer Thomas would get today from the average person who would be asked, "What is the way to heaven?"

Some might answer:

"All ways (religions) lead to heaven."

"Do the best you can, and you will make it."

"Be sincere in what you do."

"Keep the Ten Commandments."

"Go to church faithfully."

"Be baptized."

"Do good deeds."

"Nobody knows."

Jesus Christ gave the simple and sure way to heaven. He is the way. The word "way" means "road" or "path." Let me illustrate it this way. If someone were to ask you for directions to Kalamazoo from Three Rivers, you would say, "The way to get to Kalamazoo is to take road 131 and go north, and you will get to your destination." The person that needs the direction then has to get on the road that gets to the destination.

So it is with Christ who is the way to heaven. You have to receive Him and trust Him to get you to heaven. Talking about the road will not get you anywhere, and talking about

Jesus will not either. It is accepting the "way" and getting on with it that gets you there.

You may be sincere in taking a different way, and you will be sincerely wrong. Proverbs 14:12 says, "There is a way that seems right to a man, but the end thereof is the way of death."

Heaven is a wonderful place. Besides no grief, sorrow, or pain, it is a place of joy, excitement, activity, exploration, discovery; fellowship with relatives, friends, and heroes of the past; increased learning; artistic expressions; serving and ruling; receiving rewards for faithfulness on earth; and face to face with Jesus and Father God and looking your best. I could also mention space traveling to the billions of galaxies of God's created universe or visiting and recreating this new planet of ours. Wow! No wonder the Bible says in 1 Cor. 2:9, "Eye has not seen, nor ear heard, neither has it entered into the heart of man what God has prepared for those who love Him." It surely will not be boring throughout eternity.

Jesus said, "I go to prepare a place for you, that where I am there you may be also."

See you there, and I can tell you more about what heaven is like.

Rev. John Booko is the Founding Pastor of the Riverside Church.

THE PLACE OF HEAVEN

Heaven is fun—a place of unlimited pleasure, happiness, and joy (Ps. 16:11; 1 Cor. 2:9; Rev. 14:13) and filled with perfect love.
Heaven is dynamic. It is bursting with excitement and action. It is the ultimate playground. God invented it. It is Disney World, Six Flags, Hawaii, Michigan, and New York all rolled into one. It is a vacation that never ends. It is all inclusive.

We don't lose our identity in heaven (a spiritual body like Christ). Our changed body will obey the commands of the mind. (We will travel faster than light throughout God's universe.)

In heaven, we will experience a whole new variety of sights, sounds, smells, feelings, and tastes. God is a great artist and inventor and creator. Pleasurable sensations are retained in heaven, and God may substitute something better.

Our reunions and relationships in heaven are going to be fabulous (with our spouses, children, grandchildren, parents, siblings, relatives, and friends.) Even our animals. (Why not? Ps. 36:6 says God cares for people and animals alike). (Saved in the ark.) And don't forget our heavenly assistants, the angels!

"Rest in peace" means going on from what you were doing to greater things: free from worries, suffering, sickness, and pain.

Heaven will not be boring, ever! (Will it?) It will be discoveries and works that never end—with singing, dancing, playing instruments, learning to be an artist, or any other interest.

The highlight of heaven is seeing God! Worshipping and praising Him. He will then have the answers to all of our questions.

"When we all get to heaven, what a day of rejoicing that will be! When we all see Jesus, we'll sing and shout the victory!"

<u>Intro to Intro</u> (11/27/05) (Thanksgiving weekend)
1. Hi to everybody! Did you have a nice Thanksgiving? Ate a lot of Mom and Grandma's cooking? The families all got together? Great! (Every day should be a Thanksgiving Day.)

2. I read about an elderly man in Phoenix, AZ, calling his son in New York and says, "I hate to ruin your day, but I have to tell you that your mother and I are divorcing. Forty-five years of misery is enough. The son screams, "Pop, what are you talking about?" The old man says, "We can't stand the sight of each other, and I'm sick of talking about this, so call your sister in Chicago and tell her," and he hangs up. Frantic, the son calls his sister, who explodes on the phone.

She shouts, "Like heck they're getting divorced. I'll take care of this." She calls Phoenix immediately and screams at the old man. "You are NOT yelling divorced. Don't do a single thing until I get there. I'm calling brother back, and we will both be there tomorrow. Until then, don't do a thing, DO YOU HEAR ME?" And hangs up.

The old man hangs up his phone and turns to his wife and says, "Okay honey they are coming for Thanksgiving and paying their own way! Now, what do we tell them for Christmas?

3. As I told our son, Pastor Paul, about the message I am bringing today on investments and rewards, he suggested, "Dad, why don't you think about one of the great rewards that you have gotten over your eighty-three years? As I thought about it, I came up

with a great reward I received for my investment. Here she is, your mother and my wife of fifty-seven years. Burnell, Darling, stand up and take a wave!

INVESTMENTS AND REWARDS ("What's in it for me?")
(Video parody on meism in church)

Intr.: You hear a lot these days about:

1. Financial planning, financial planners, stock markets, investments, and saving for retirement. (Financial planners Ameriprise & Weiser & Associates, our grandsons and son in them.) (Why do they call the person who invests all of our money "a broker"?) (Talk about investing.)

   1) I was told that a person earning $20,000 annually and setting aside 10 percent with a financial planner at age twenty, when that person is sixty years old, he could be a millionaire! (Setting aside only $166 per month!)c(Based on average return since 1929) ($1,200,000–1,534,000 at 12 percent returns) (Ben Frugal Franklin said, "If you want to double your money, fold it.")

   2) Noah, the greatest financier in the Bible, floated his stock while the world was in liquidation.

2. What about the investments for eternal life? (Life after death)

3. I want to talk to new and old believers and seekers and YP now.

   1) What do you get out of being a follower of Jesus Christ? (Besides getting eternal life in heaven, what more is there?)

2) Apostle Peter asked this same question of Christ in Matt. 19:27.

   (1) What kind of a question is this?

   (2) What will Jesus say? (Shame on you?)

3) Here is what Jesus answered to the question, "What's in it for us?" (Matt. 19:28, 29). (What a return on your investment! 10,000%)

4. INVESTING YOUR CHRISTIAN LIFE IN GOD'S KINGDOM PROMISES GREAT REWARDS FOR THE INVESTMENT (OF YOUR LIFE) (AS SURE AS THERE IS A HEAVEN, THERE ARE REWARDS THERE!) (HERE ON EARTH ALSO!) SOME PERKS

What's in it for you?

I. REWARDS!

   1. 2 Cor. 5:10. (This is different from the great white throne judgment of the lost sinners in Rev. 20:11, 15) (for degree of punishment)

   2. 1 Cor. 3:11–15 – At the judgment seat of Christ

Get the picture? Every Christian is building with life.

1) Building materials, 12 (That which is good or not good)

2) Materials tested, 13

3) Rewards promised, 14

4) Losses endured, 15 (Some disappointed, some surprised) (Illus. Preacher dreamed of going to heaven and expecting a real nice crown; it was given to the little widow lady who prayed for him as he would preach.)

5) Let's talk about these materials that we use for building a life upon Christ: Wood, hay, and

straw are not good (made up of hatred, lies, unforgiveness, immoral acts, prideful acts, disobedience to God's word, and breaking God's commands). Gold, silver, and precious stones are good stuff—giving God your time, talents, and treasures (made up of prayer, Bible reading, church attendance, obeying God's word, doing good, serving others, being led by the Holy Spirit, etc.). ("Only one life, 'twill soon be past. Only what's done for Christ will last." A motto I saw.)

5. This is not to earn salvation to heaven; you already have that by receiving Christ as your Savior (Eph. 2:8). (Salvation is not a reward; it is a gift!)

6. The "T" formation of Time, Talent, and Treasure for the Lord brings a great inheritance reward (Col. 3:23, 24).
   1) Time: Out of 168 hours in a week, how much for God? (Prayer, Bible, church, serving God, etc.) Invest.
   2) Talent: God has given it to be used for His glory. (See "opportunities - volunteer list in the bulletin.) (Look and see or ask.)
   3) Treasure: Tithes and offerings (You can't take your money with you, but you could send it on ahead.)
      (1) Think of tithes and offerings as a glorious investment in God's kingdom.
      (2) Jesus said we would get 100 times for what we gave up. What a return on our investment: Example of average income of 30,000 per year; tithe 3,000 plus 1,000 offerings: total from age 20 to 80; $240,000 x 60 yrs., at 100 times (or

10,000%) = $2,4000,000,000. What a return on our investment!

II. <u>YOU WANT CROWNS?</u> (There are at least five of them. For your investment in heaven!)

1. Crown or self-discipline (self-control) (<u>1 Cor. 9:25–27)</u>
2. Crown of life – for enduring trials (James <u>1:12)</u> (Faithfulness, Rev. 2:10)
3. Crown of glory – for faithful service as a church leader (<u>1 Pet. 5:1–4)</u>
4. Crown of joy – for helping lead others to Christ (You did this by praying, giving, inviting, and living an attractive life.) (<u>1 Thess. 2:19)</u> (NKJV says "crown of rejoicing")
5. Crown of righteousness – for loving Christ's second coming (<u>2 Tim. 4:7, 8)</u>

(Jesus said we would <u>reign with him</u>; crowns for authority fit in with this.)

(Someone said, "I'm going to lay my crowns at the feet of Jesus!)

CONCL:

1. How do you like this eternal life investment and returns?
2. Through eternity, we Christians will have with us only the things which we did for God while here on earth. That's why Jesus said (<u>Matt. 6:19–21).</u>
3. Laboring for God is not in vain (<u>1 Cor. 15:58)</u> (Others' labors may be in vain, like a lawyer or a doctor, but not working for God.)

4. The bottom line though is <u>2 Cor. 5:14</u>, "Christ's love <u>compels</u> us." (But the rewards <u>excite</u> us as God has promised them for our invested lives.)

5. When I see Jesus in heaven, I wish to hear him say this to me and to you: <u>Matt. 25:21</u>.

6. Prayer: I pray:

    1) For those <u>not yet</u> on the foundation of Jesus Christ to build upon. For open eyes and hearts to ask Christ to come in. (WILL YOU DO IT JUST NOW? TELL HIM YOU WANT HIM AS YOUR FRIEND.)

    2) For those of us building our lives on Christ that we will not be weary in doing well. As you have said, "At the proper time, we shall reap a harvest if we do not give up."

    3) To you, Father God, be all the glory for our investment through Jesus Christ our Lord and Savior. Amen!

<u>21m</u>
(stretch 4m for 25m)
(went to 35, 11/05)

Scripture for Message on Investments and Rewards: (NIV)

<u>Intr.</u>

3.2- Matt. 19:27 – Peter answered him (Jesus), "We have left everything to follow you! What then will there be for us?"

3.3- Matt. 19:28, 29 – Jesus said to them, "I tell you the truth, at the renewal of all things, when the Son of Man sits on his glorious throne, you who have followed me will also sit on twelve thrones judging the twelve tribes of Israel. And <u>everyone</u> who has left houses or brothers or sisters or father or mother or children or fields for my sake will receive a hundred times as much . . ."

I. 1. 2 Cor. 5:10 – For we must all appear before the judgment seat of Christ, that each one may receive what is due him for the things done while in the body, whether good or bad.

(Rev. 20:11, 15 – Then I saw a great white throne and him who was seated on it. If anyone's name was not found written in the book of life, he was thrown into the lake of fire.)

I. 2. 1 Cor. 3:11–15 – For no one can lay any foundation other than the one already laid, which is Christ Jesus, If any man builds on this foundation using gold, silver, costly stones, wood, hay or straw, his work will be shown for what it is, because the Day will bring it to light. It will be revealed by fire, and the fire will test the quality of each man's work. If what he has built survives, he will receive his <u>reward</u>. If it is burned up, he will suffer <u>loss</u>; he himself will be <u>saved</u>, but only as one escaping through the flames.

I. 5.   Eph. 2:8 – For it is by grace you have been saved, through faith—and not of yourselves, it is the gift of God—<u>not by works</u>, so that no one can boast.

I. 6.   Col. 3:23, 24 – Whatever you do, work at it with all your heart, as working for the Lord and not men, since you know that you will receive an inheritance from the Lord as a reward. It is the Lord Christ you are serving.

II. 1. 1 Cor. 9:25–27 – Everyone who competes in the games goes into strict training. They do it to get <u>a crown</u> that will not last; but we do it to get a crown that will last forever. Therefore I do not run like a man running aimlessly, I do not fight like a man beating the air. No, <u>I beat my body and make it my slave</u> that after I have preached to others, I myself will not be disqualified for <u>the prize.</u>

2.   James 1:12 – Blessed is the man who <u>perseveres under trial,</u> because when he has stood the test, he will receive <u>the crown of life</u> that God has promised to those who love him.

3.   1 Peter 5:1–4 – To the elders among you . . . <u>Be shepherds of God's flock that is under your care</u> . . . And when the Chief Shepherd appears, you will receive <u>the crown of glory</u> that will never fade away.

4.   1 Thess. 2:19 – For what is our hope, our joy, or <u>the crown in which we glory</u> in the presence of our Lord Jesus when he comes? <u>Is it not you?</u>

5.   2 Tim. 4:7, 8 – I have fought a good fight, I have finished the race, I have kept the faith. Now there is in store for me <u>the crown of righteousness</u>, which the Lord, the righteous Judge, will award me on that day—and not only to me but also <u>to all who have longed for his appearing.</u>

<u>Concl.</u>

2.   Matt. 6:19–21 - Do not store up for yourselves treasures on earth, where moth and rust destroy, and where thieves break through and steal. But store up for yourselves treasures in heaven . . . For where your treasure is, there will your heart be also.

3.   1 Cor. 15:58 – Always give yourselves fully to the work of the Lord, because you know that your labor in the Lord is not in vain.

4.   2 Cor. 5:14 – For Christ's love compels us . . .

5.   Matt. 25:21 – His master replied, "Well done, good and faithful servant? You have been faithful with a few things; I will put you <u>in charge of many things</u>. Come and share with master's happiness."

EVERLASTING LIFE: "And he that believeth not the Son shall not see life; but the wrath of God abideth on him" (John 3:36).

DO YOU KNOW THE WAY TO HEAVEN YET?

It is not by joining any church, nor being baptized, nor doing good deeds. Many may go to heaven:

"Without health
Without wealth
Without fame
Without a great name
Without learning
Without big earnings
Without culture
Without beauty
Without friends
Without ten thousand other things, BUT
NONE GO TO HEAVEN WITHOUT CHRIST."

It is only through Christ who said: "I am the Way, the Truth, and the Life, no man cometh unto the Father, but by Me" (John 14:6).

Receive Christ now as your personal Savior and Lord of your life; follow His teachings in the Bible, and you will be able to say as King David said in the Psalm: "Surely goodness and mercy shall follow me all the days of my life: and I WILL DWELL IN THE HOUSE OF THE LORD FOREVER."

<u>HEAVEN</u>

THE PLACE

THE PREPARATION

THE PROMISE

THE PEOPLE

BY REV. JOHN BOOKO

HEAVEN

A little girl was gazing at the sky one clear night. Her father asked her, "At what are you staring, my dear?" She answered, "Oh daddy, I was just thinking that if the bottom side of heaven is so beautiful, how wonderful it must be on the other side."

HEAVEN MUST BE WONDERFUL

It is a comfort for folks to know there is a heaven to go to. Death does not end all.

Jesus comforted His disciples with the thought of heaven when they were sad and discouraged about His coming death. He said: "Let not your heart be troubled: ye believe in God, believe also in me. In my Father's house are many mansions: if it were not so I would have told you. I go to prepare a place for you. And if I go and prepare a place for you, I will come again, and receive you unto myself; that where I am, there ye may be also" (John 14:1–3).

CHRIST TELLS US THE FACTS ABOUT HEAVEN.

1. THE PLACE

Heaven is somewhere in particular and not just everywhere in general. Heaven is the place where God dwells.—"In my Father's house" (John 14:2). We say in the Model Prayer: "Our Father who art in heaven...."

Heaven is the place where Christ has gone. Jesus arose in a body of flesh and bone, ascended into heaven, and is now living in heaven in that body. The angels testified of this to the disciples in Acts 1:10, 11. "And while they looked steadfastly toward heaven as he went up, behold, two men stood by them in white apparel; Which also said, Ye men of Galilee, why stand ye gazing up into heaven? this same Jesus, which is taken up from you into heaven, shall so come in like manner as ye have seen him go into heaven."

Those who have died in Christ are now "absent from the body and present with the Lord" (2 Cor. 5:8). They are with the Lord in heaven.

2. THE PREPARATIONS

Heaven is being prepared for the Christians by Christ—"I go to prepare a place for you." There are many "mansions" or abiding places for us. Someone has said that if Christ could make the beautiful world that we live in six days, what must heaven be like where Christ has been preparing it for us for over nineteen hundred years?

3. THE PROMISE

"I will come again." "To receive you unto Myself." "That where I am, there ye may be also." We "born again" Christians will be with Jesus the Savior. We shall see Him face to face. "Face to face with Christ my Savior, Face to face––what will it be––When with rapture I behold Him, Jesus Christ who died for me? Face to face I shall behold Him, Far beyond the starry sky; Face to face in all His glory, I shall see Him by and by!" And with Him, we shall see all of our saved loved ones. IT'S A PROMISE!

4. THE PEOPLE

We must be a prepared people. We must be ready for heaven while on earth. Jesus tells us that only those who have been "born again" through receiving Christ as Savior and Lord are the prepared people for heaven. "Verily, verily, I say unto thee, Except a man be born again, he cannot see the kingdom of God" (John 3:3).

These prepared people must have the promise of God while living that eternal life in heaven is theirs. And we can know! "These things have I written unto you that believe in the name of the Son of God; that ye may KNOW that ye have eternal life" (1 John 5:13). The promise is given to all who accept Christ as personal Savior and Lord. "But as many as received him, to them gave he power (authority) to become the sons of God" (John 1:12).

"And this is the record, that God hath given to us eternal life, and this life is in his Son. He that hath the Son hath life; and he that hath not the Son of God hath not life" (1 John 5:11, 12). "He that believeth on the Son HATH

"BORN AGAIN"

As the Scripture

Speaks of It.

TO ENTER HEAVEN

REV. JOHN BOOKO
200 S. HOOKER AVE
THREE RIVERS MI 49093

"BORN AGAIN"

As the Scripture Speaks of It

It is wonderful to be saved, isn't it? Have you ever made an inventory of what one does have when he is saved, converted, "born again," as the scripture speaks of it? Think of it! Sins are forgiven when one is saved; one has a new nature, has a Father in heaven, and promises of answered prayers. This does not mean that those who are not Christians do not get answered prayers. They may get a few of them answered by God's grace. They do not have the promise of answered prayers as those who are saved. Those who are saved have eternal life. They have love and joy.

I would like to pause for half a minute on joy. I said, "Those who are saved have joy." If there is anything that does not attract someone else to Christ, it is the long, sour, sad face of one who calls himself a Christian. One of the greatest hindrances to the Christian life is a sad face because the Christian has joy. If you are a Christian and you do not have joy on your face, why don't you have your heart notify your face about it and have joy?

One who is saved also has peace. The Holy Spirit is in the life of the Christian. The soul is saved. There is the promise of resurrection and eternity in heaven. These uncalculated riches and many more belong to the one who is saved and has become a child of God.

Longfellow, it is said, could take a worthless sheet of paper, write a poem on it, and make it worth $6,000. That's genius! Rockefeller could sign his name on a piece of paper and make it worth $1,000,000. That's capital! Uncle Sam takes silver, stamps it, and makes it worth a dollar. That's money! A mechanic takes material worth $5 and makes an article worth $50 out of it. That's skill! An artist can take a piece of canvas, paint a picture on it, and make it worth $1,000. That's art! God can take a worthless sinful life, wash it in the blood of Christ, put his Spirit in it, and make it a blessing to humanity. That's salvation!

Now to become a child of God, one must accept Christ as his personal savior. We want to emphasize this truth, to those who may not be sure that they are saved. This should be emphasized for Christians, so that they may know what is necessary in speaking to someone without Christ. The Bible says that in order to become a child of God one must accept Christ as personal Savior and Lord. We find in John 1:12 that it has the term "Received Him." "Receiving Him" is a term expressing this truth of the need of accepting Christ as savior. To those who received Him (Christ), He gave the power to become the sons of God.

The word "receive" is a passive term. When you do nothing, you are passive. The word "receive" in the Bible is in the active voice (in the Greek) when you do the act. It is not passive. Those who receive Him can see that there is some action involved. To them, He gave the power or right or authority to become the sons of God. So you see this doesn't mean simply believing the information about Christ. There are too many church members who feel that they are saved because they believe in their mind some information about Christ. That is passive. Believing is passive. You can believe things and not do anything. That is not receiving, and one becomes a child of God, remember, by receiving Him.

To illustrate this point, I have just given, how intellectual assent, or believing something, really doesn't get you anywhere, I would like to have you think with me about a trip that I might want to take to Chicago. I call the Grand Trunk Depot and ask the man when the train is going to be leaving for Chicago. He gives me the time and I go at that time, say three o'clock in the afternoon, and purchase a ticket. This ticket is for the train that takes me to Chicago. Soon the train pulls into the station, some people get off and some get on. You ask there, "Are you going to Chicago?" "Yes, this is the train that is going to Chicago." You ask the conductor. "Is this train going to Chicago?" "Yes." You have got the ticket, you believe all these things, and your faith is strong in the fact that this train goes to Chicago. All of a sudden, the train starts to pull away and you are still there at the depot believing all of these things. Yes, you believe all of these facts about that train and you even have your ticket, but you are not on the way to Chicago because you have had this passive belief. One may believe all these creeds about Jesus Christ and say, "Yes, I believe that Jesus Christ died for the world and His blood was shed on the cross," but unless you receive him and he receives you at the same time, you don't get to Heaven.

That is in the Bible. Just as you don't get to Chicago unless you get on that train, until you receive it and it receives you. This is what is meant by believing in Christ. We have heard too much "easy believism" in the past where there are many persons who think they are saved but they are not; that all you have to do is believe. The demons believe, tremble, the Bible says, and are not saved. I'm afraid that is why we don't have many out and out Christians, witnessing Christians, because they haven't had this active believing and receiving. Now to prove beyond a shadow of a doubt that believing is receiving, God has put those two words in this one verse. "As many as **received** Him, (Christ,) to them gave He power to become the sons of God, even to them that **believe** on His name," which means, in the end, that those who are receiving, are the ones who are doing the real believing. So this is one term the Bible names, expressing this truth of the need of accepting Christ as personal Savior and Lord.

There is another term, "letting Him come in" (Rev. 3:20). Jesus says, "Behold I stand at the door and knock, if any man hear my voice and open the door I will come in to him and will sup with him and he with Me." Christ is pictured as knocking at our life's door, wanting to be let in. "Behold I stand at the door," the life and heart, and He knocks. He knocks, but He does not break open the door. We again have to be the active agent. If we do nothing, He will not come in. We have to be active. "If any man hear my voice and open the door" (There it is -- activity). He will come in. He knocks at our heart's door in many ways. He is knocking right now by His words. When one hears the Word of God, that is God knocking at that one's life, wanting entrance. He also knocks in His providence or in various circumstances. I find one of the most effective ways the Lord knocks: when persons do not listen to His word is when He really knocks them on their backs. When they are knocked on their backs, say by an accident, they have a chance to really think about the Lord and say, "Why, what do the material things in this life matter?" You work at two jobs and work **your** head off trying to accumulate the necessary material things. One doesn't have time for the spiritual things, and he is knocked flat on his back, and it dawns on him, "Why, what good is all of the material now?" Sometimes, God has to bring **you** to that point where you see that the things of this world don't really count, and only having Christ is what counts. He knocks in His various ways to enter into your life. We have to let Him come in to be saved. If Christ is kept outside, something must be wrong inside. Christ comes in when we open the door. He says He stands at the door knocking. If any man hears His voice and opens the door, He will come in. That is one of the best verses for assurance of being saved. That is one of the best ways one can know that he is saved, by having faith in this verse. Notice what Christ said. If anyone hears His voice and opens the door, He will come in. No one who opens the heart's door to Christ needs to question whether Christ came in because He said He would, didn't He? All we have to do is open the door. He will do the rest. He will do His part of coming in.

Many times when I have the wonderful privilege of leading someone to Christ, I ask the person, "Are you saved?" The person says, "Yes," and I say, "Suppose someone were to ask you, 'How do you know you're saved?'" Now the most frequent answer is, "Well, I feel really good inside," and I say, "That is wonderful. You should feel good, but if you're basing your assurance that you're saved on how good you feel, what if you wake up the next morning and you don't feel too good? You might feel a little sick––maybe a little indigestion, and you just don't feel very good––then what's going to happen to your assurance if you're depending on how you feel?"

And I say, "Now let's look at this verse, Rev. 3:20. You opened your heart's door to Christ," and the person says, "Yes." "What did Christ say He would do? Christ says, 'I will come in.' Now according to this verse, how do you know Christ came into your life?" Sometimes they still don't get it, and after pressing so that they may get hold of that truth, it dawns on them that the reason they may know they're saved and Christ came in is because **He said He would,** and He cannot lie, and that is our assurance that We're saved.

There is a true story about a home where someone left an almanac at the door of a little cottage. In the center of this almanac was a picture of the Lord Jesus knocking at the door of hearts. Some of you have a picture of Christ knocking at the door. This was like that. The mother hung this almanac in the kitchen, and when the little boy came home from school, he asked about it. But mother was getting supper ready, and she didn't take time to answer his questions, and pretty soon his father came in, and the boy said, "Daddy, who's knocking at the door?" And the father said, "Well, that's Jesus knocking at the door." The little boy said, "Why is He knocking at the door?" The father didn't answer the question, and the boy kept asking about it, "Why is Jesus knocking at the door?" Finally, the father said, "He wants to get in." This father, unsaved, answered him shortly and didn't go into it anymore, and the boy said, "Why don't they let Him come in?" Dinner came, and the father changed the subject, and again and again, this little heart was touched by that scene in that incident, and he kept asking, "Why don't they let Him in?" Soon that question was ringing in this father's ears and in the father's heart. At last, two days later, this father fell on his knees and cried, "Lord Jesus, I know you are knocking at my heart. Please forgive me for keeping you outside and keeping you waiting so long. Lord Jesus, the door is open. Won't you come in right now?" And Christ came in and saved that father and used him in that home. Jesus said, "I stand at the door and knock. If any man hears my voice and opens the door, I will come in to him and sup with him and he with me."

Now the third term that I want to mention, emphasizing the same thing, the need of accepting Christ the Savior, is the term "taking Him." Rev. 22:17 says, "And the Spirit and the Bride Say, Come. And let him that heareth, say Come. And let him that is athirst come. And whosoever will, let him take the water of life freely." Taking the water of life is taking Christ. This expresses the truth of the need of accepting Him, the Savior. A thirsty man must take the water in order to have his thirst quenched. Christ said that if we come to Him and drink, we will have our spiritual thirst quenched, and we will have the Holy Spirit in us. Water is also the symbol of the Spirit, and when the Bible says, "Take the water of Life," this again shows the need of doing something about Christ in order to have the promised result. Doing something about it! Taking Him—not just looking at Him. Not just believing about Him, but taking Him into the life and having a relationship made. I want to illustrate this matter of taking Christ as Savior by a personal illustration, and you will know what I'm talking about because it's happened to some of you. There was a time I was introduced to a young lady, and I thought she was a nice girl, and we chatted for a few minutes at a church party. We happened to see each other again on Sunday, and we talked a little more. Soon I found that I was deeply interested in that young lady in more than a friendly way, for I began to build a kind of belief about her, you might say. I began to believe she was a very sincere Christian. I began to believe she possessed qualities and abilities God could use in His service. I began to believe her tastes were very similar to mine, and I began to believe that, incredible as it was, she really liked me, and I began to believe that I was falling in love. Now in my mind, I had this long creed and belief about that girl, and I subscribed to that creed honestly, and yet that creed, that belief, made no difference regarding our personal relationship until there came that never forgotten time in church when I said, as we exchanged our marriage vows, "I take thee to be my wife." That definite act, when I said, "I take thee to be my wife," established a life-transforming relationship when I became her husband, and every other relationship was altered when I took that person. That is the way it is with Jesus Christ. Again, there may be a lot of belief about Him; you may even say you love Him, but you have to take Him into your life and say, "I take you as my Savior and Lord," which involves responsibilities. "I take you as my Savior and Lord." Lord means Lord of the life when one makes the decision. On that basis, then, a relationship is established just as in marriage. We assumed quite a responsibility from then on that we didn't have before. It comes from taking something, someone, that changes our relationship, and any others are forever altered.

Now, have you accepted Christ as your personal Savior and Lord? You are not a child of God in the spiritual sense until you do so, for the Word of God which I have been giving you, says, "As many as received Him, to them, (the ones who receive) gave He power (or the right) to become the sons of God" (or children of God). No one else is a child of God but the one who receives Christ as Savior.

Salvation is a gift. Now, what two actions can one take when offered a gift? "The wages of sin is death, but the gift of God is eternal life through Jesus Christ our Lord." A gift––what two actions can you take? Either receive or refuse. It's as simple as that––to receive or refuse. There are these only two alternatives in this matter of receiving Christ. One receives or refuses, and one who does not receive Christ cannot say, "Well, I'm not rejecting Him." Yes, the one who has not received Christ is rejecting Christ. If you had a gift and you were to offer it to someone, if that person did not receive that gift, that person's action, that person just being passive, will tell you he or she is rejecting that gift. And so, you may make no move to accept Christ the Savior, but by that very act, you show that for the present, you are rejecting Him. And why would someone reject Jesus Christ the Savior, who gives us salvation, which, the Bible said, brings us all those riches which we talked about earlier? It doesn't make sense, does it, that persons are rejecting the Savior in this country of ours? But they are. It seems incredible that they are rejecting Christ when so much could be theirs by accepting Him. It is much worse than the news item that came from Belleville, Illinois, where the stunt Belleville National Bank had featured the celebration of its silver jubilee. This bank gave the radio announcer, Bill Bailey, forty silver dollars and authorized him to sell them at fifty cents each. He was equipped with his portable microphone, and he roamed the block in front of the bank for thirty minutes. His approach was to offer a silver dollar in his outstretched hand and just ask, "Will you give me fifty cents for this silver dollar?" His first potential customer was an elderly retired farmer, and he examined the coin gingerly and scrutinized the date and handed it back with a glare, and said, "I think you are a racketeer from St. Louis," and he hurried away. The next man approached by Bill Bailey recoiled and threatened to call a policeman. A housewife did make the first purchase and she said, "It looks like a good deal to me," and she opened her purse for fifty cents and said, "In these times, I'm willing to take a chance on anything." Another woman told Bailey hesitantly, "I've only got a quarter," and another woman pushed the price down to eleven cents before buying it. But after the program, and this was being broadcast on the radio, Bailey turned back thirty-six unused silver dollars. Before calling the people of Belleville foolish for hesitating to purchase silver dollars at half price, stop and ask yourself if you are not doing something even more foolish in refusing to accept the Lord's offer of eternal life as a free gift. Strangely enough, because it's a free gift, some people think there is a catch to it, and I've heard them say that it seems that it's just too cheap, this being saved through receiving Christ the Savior. But the Scripture says, "The gift of God is eternal life through Jesus Christ our Lord."

I want to close with a wonderful letter of witness a girl sent to a G. I. This G. I. had received a blood transfusion, and it saved his life. The blood donor's name was sent with this blood, and he wrote her a letter of thanks. She wrote this letter back that so well emphasized this truth and fact of receiving Christ the Savior. She wrote, "Dear G. I. Joe, How nice of you to write a personal letter of thanks for the help my Red Cross blood donation was to you. We can both thank God that blood was on hand when and where you needed it. I trust your strength will be returning rapidly and that someday soon, I may meet you back home. In the meantime, I am wondering if you have ever expressed your thanks for a blood donation far more costly and needful than any I could give. I mean, of course, the precious blood which Christ gave for the sins of the world 2,000 years ago. What a gift it is. While mine to you caused only brief inconvenience, His gift cost untold agony. I gave what I could easily spare. He gave His life to die and rise again, that lost men might be saved from their sins. My blood helped prolong your physical life. How thankful I am it did, but because of His death and resurrection for you, you can have eternal life. My blood helped heal your body; His heals and cleanses the soul. Mine aided you only, but His is effective for all of the world. In one respect His gift and mine are similar, both must be accepted personally. My blood helped you only when you received it. Christ's sacrifice for you will not give you spiritual life unless you accept Him as your Savior. I know it would have seemed unthinkable when you were in desperate need to have refused the blood I was so glad to send your way. I trust that it will seem far more unthinkable to refuse His gift, given with much greater love to meet an infinitely greater need. I would be so glad to hear that you have done this and are trusting Christ as your savior. Sincerely yours, Wilma Hiscock."

Yes, "as many as received Him, to them gave He power to become the sons of God, even to them that believe on His name. Behold, I stand at the door and knock. If any man hear my voice and open the door, I will come into him. And the Spirit and the Bride Say, Come. And let him that is athirst come. And whosoever will, let him take the water of life freely."

Shall we bow our heads in prayer?

Dear God, thank You for Your love and the gift of salvation through Your Son, Jesus Christ.

I realize that I am a sinner and that Jesus Christ died for me so that I may be saved from my sins and from hell and for heaven.

I turn away from the devil and my sinful ways and turn to Christ to receive Him as my Savior and Lord of my life.

Thank You for the assurance of Your Word that in doing this I am saved and born again by Your Holy Spirit who comes into my life now.

I yield completely to Jesus Christ now to be filled with Your Holy Spirit. I want to be a devoted follower of Christ by obeying Your words in the Bible.

Praise be to You, Lord, now and forever. Amen

Printed in the United States
by Baker & Taylor Publisher Services